We the People

Student Text

Center for Civic Education

5146 Douglas Fir Road ■ Calabasas, CA 91302–1467 ■ (818) 591-9321
Fax (818) 591-9330 ■ wethepeople@civiced.org ■ http://www.civiced.org

Directed by the

Center for Civic Education

and

Funded by the

U.S. Department of Education by act of Congress

Established 1987 under the

Commission on the Bicentennial of the United States Constitution

Cover: "Stump Speaking," George Caleb Bingham
Art Collection of The Boatmen's National Bank of St. Louis

ISBN 0-89818-108-9

Acknowledgments

The following staff and consultants have contributed to the development of this text.

Editorial Directors
Charles N. Quigley
Duane E. Smith
Jane G. Sure

General Editor
Judith A. Matz

Production Directors
Kerin Martin
Theresa Richard

Staff Associates
John Hale
Michael Leong
Gary Mickens
Howard Safier

Consulting Associates
Phyllis Clarke
Gloria Eastman
Tom Fitzgerald
Barbara Miller
Eugenia Moore
David Morgan
Laurel Singleton
John Zola

Typesetters
Roslyn Danberg
Jan Ruyle

Production Assistants
Lise Borja
Anne Drooker
Pat Mathwig
Steve Wasserman

Illustrations and Graphics
Richard Stein

The Center is also grateful for the many helpful comments and suggestions that have been received from the following persons who have reviewed the manuscript in its various developmental stages. The Center has attempted to be responsive to all of the many valuable suggestions for improvement in the text. However, the final product is the responsibility of the Center and does not necessarily reflect the views of those who have contributed their thoughts and ideas.

Margaret Branson, Administrator
Division of Instructional Services
Kern County Public Schools
Kern Country, California

Gary Bryner, Professor
Department of Political Science
Brigham Young University

Maria Cedeno, Teacher
Citrus Grove Middle School
Miami, Florida

Stephen Feinberg
Social Studies Curriculum Leader
Wayland Junior High School
Wayland, Massachusetts

James R. Giese
Executive Director
Social Science Education
  Consortium, Inc.
Boulder, Colorado

Jack N. Hoar, Consultant
Long Beach Unified Schools
Long Beach, California

John LaGore
Magnet Program Specialist
McKinley School
Bakersfield, California

Karen Levine, Teacher
Brooklawn Junior High School
Parsippany Hills, New Jersey

Paula Lieb, Teacher
Churchill Junior High School
East Brunswick, New Jersey

Gary Marksbury
Mentor Teacher/Department Head
Hughes Junior High School
Lakewood, California

Lynn McDonald, Teacher
Groveport, Ohio

Dana Mills, Teacher
Longfellow Junior High
Enid, Oklahoma

Henry Mueller, Coordinator
Middle School Social Studies
Niskayuna Central School District
Niskayuna, New York

Sue Olds
Social Science Department Chair
Holmes Junior High School
Davis, California

Evelyn Richman
Coordinator, Law Program
JHS 166
Brooklyn, New York

Joel Rosen, Teacher
P.S. 99
Brooklyn, New York

Janet Russell
Social Studies Department Head
Shotwell Middle School
Houston, Texas

W.A. "Del" Stelck
Professor Emeritus
Department of History
California State University
Northridge, California

Judy Wolff
Teacher/Department Chair
Mulholland Junior High School
Van Nuys, California

Members of the Commission on the
Bicenntennial of the United States Constitution

Advisory Committee
The Citizen and the Constitution

Board or Directors
Center for Civic Education

Warren E. Burger (1907–1995)
Chief Justice of the United States, 1969–1986
Chairman, Commission on the Bicentennial of the United States Constitution

The years 1987 to 1991 marked the 200th anniversary of the writing, ratification, and implementation of the basic documents of American democracy, the Constitution and the Bill of Rights. Our Constitution has stood the tests and stresses of time, wars and change. Although it was not perfect, as Benjamin Franklin and many others recognized, it has lasted because it was carefully crafted by men who understood the importance of a system of government sufficiently strong to meet the challenges of the day, yet sufficiently flexible to accommodate and adapt to new political, economic, and social conditions. Many Americans have but a slight understanding of the Constitution, the Bill of Rights, and the later amendments to which we pledge our allegiance. The lessons in this book are designed to give you, the next generation of American citizens, an understanding of the background, creation, and subsequent history of the unique system of government brought into being by our Constitution. At the same time, it will help you understand the principles and ideals that underlie and give meaning to the Constitution, a system of government by those governed.

Table of Contents

Introduction

This book is not like most history books. Most history books tell the story of people and events of the past. This book is a **history of ideas**. It explains the most important ideas of our Constitution and tells how they were developed. It also tells about the people and events that were important in the history of these ideas.

The Constitution of the United States was written in Philadelphia 200 years ago. It was a plan for a new government for our country. We need to study the Constitution and its history to understand our government and how it is supposed to work. Knowing our past will help us understand the rights and responsibilities that we have today.

In this book, you will discover what the men who wrote our Constitution thought the purposes of government should be. They believed government should protect our lives, liberty, and property. They also believed government should promote the common welfare. You will also learn why they thought it was necessary to limit the powers of government.

You will learn about some of the things that have happened to the Constitution since it was written in 1787. You will study ways in which it has changed and how these changes came about. You will also learn about ways the Constitution has stayed the same.

We hope this book will help you develop a good understanding of the Constitution and our system of government. It should also help you understand more about how our government affects your life and how you can influence your government.

Unit One: What is government?

What do you know about the Framers of our Constitution?

Purpose of Unit One

Fifty-five men met in Philadelphia in the summer of 1787. They wrote our Constitution. These men knew a great deal about government. They, and many other Americans, had learned about government in at least three ways.

1. They had read and discussed books about basic ideas of government written by political philosophers. A **political philosopher** is a person who studies and writes about basic ideas about government. For example, a philosopher might write about the idea of freedom and why freedom is important. Or, he or she might write about the best way to organize a government to protect basic rights.

2. They had read and discussed books about the history of governments over the past 2,000 years. From these books they learned what types of governments had worked well and had helped people live well. They also learned what types of governments had oppressed people and violated their rights.

3. They had had experiences with government themselves. Many had been leaders in the governments of the American colonies when they were ruled by Great Britain. And many had been leaders in the governments of the new states formed after our nation had freed itself of British rule.

The men who wrote the Constitution were not the only people in America at that time who knew a lot about government. More people in America knew how to read and write than in any other country in the world. Many Americans had read the writings of political philosophers and historians. Others had at least heard about some of their main ideas about government from sermons, popular pamphlets, and newspapers.

Americans had not only read about government, they were experienced in governing themselves. Americans had been largely self-governing for over one hundred fifty years before the Revolution. After they had declared their independence from Great Britain, they had written constitutions for their new states. They had then governed those states under their new constitutions.

The men who wrote the Constitution used their knowledge and experience to create the best kind of government they could. Understanding their knowledge and experience will help you understand why they created the kind of government we have today. It will also help you understand the most important ideas they included in our Constitution.

Unit One will help you understand some of the most important ideas from political philosophy included in the Declaration of Independence, the Constitution, and the Bill of Rights. These are the ideas of natural rights, republicanism, and constitutionalism. It is important to understand these ideas because they provide a foundation for understanding the rest of the lessons in this book.

Unit Two will help you understand some of the most important historic events and experiences that affected the way the new Constitution was written.

Throughout the book, the most important ideas and terms used in each lesson are listed at the beginning of the lesson. These ideas and terms are defined in the lesson itself or in the glossary at the end of the book.

In this book, the word **Founders** means the men and women who lived in America during the colonial period who influenced the creation of our government. The word **Framers** means the men who wrote our Constitution in 1787 at the Philadelphia Convention. For example, John Adams, Mercy Otis Warren, Thomas Paine, Patrick Henry, and Thomas Jefferson were Founders. They were not Framers, because they did not attend the Philadelphia Convention.

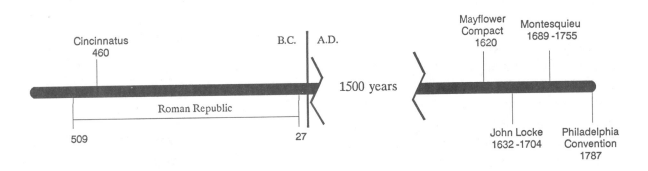

What other events can you add to this timeline?

Why do we need a government?

Purpose of Lesson

This lesson introduces you to some of the basic ideas which were of great importance to the Founders. They used these ideas when they developed our government. You will learn why they thought we need a government in the first place. You will also learn how they believed governments should be created and what they ought to do.

Terms to know

natural rights
government
absolute power
state of nature
consent
social compact or social contract

Problem solving

Identifying basic rights

Think of a right you believe all people should have. For example, you probably agree that everyone in the United States has the right to be protected from robbers and burglars. The belief that everyone should have this protection is shared by most people in the United States. It is often discussed on television and in the newspapers.

Individually or in small groups, explain how you think rights like the one you have identified can be protected.

What were the main ideas of Locke's philosophy?

Defining "natural rights"

Most people in the American colonies believed that everyone had a right to life, liberty, and property. These rights were called **natural rights**. (Sometimes these are now called basic rights or fundamental rights.) The idea of natural rights means that all persons have these rights just because they are human beings. Everyone is born with these rights and they should not be taken away without a person's agreement.

Many of the Founders believed people receive these rights from God. Others believed that people have them just because it is natural for people to have them.

John Locke was a famous English philosopher. He lived from 1632 to 1704. He had written a book called *Two Treatises of Civil Government* (1690). In that book he wrote about natural rights. He said that the

4

main purpose of **government** should be to protect the people's natural rights. He also said that kings should not have **absolute power,** that is, power without limits. They should not be able to deprive people of their natural rights.

Many Americans had read Locke's book, and they agreed with what it said about government. Those who had not actually read Locke's book knew his ideas from newspapers, political pamphlets, church sermons, and discussions.

Protecting natural rights

Although people agreed on certain natural rights, they worried about how those rights could be protected. Locke and others thought about what life would be like in a situation where there was no government and no laws. They called this situation a **state of nature.** They were afraid that in a state of nature their rights would be taken away.

How does this drawing illustrate the idea of "state of nature"? What natural rights are being violated?

5

Compare your list with John Locke's

You may have seen the same disadvantages in a state of nature that John Locke saw. Locke believed:

1. Stronger and smarter people might try to take away other people's lives, liberty, or property.

2. Weaker people might band together and take away the rights of the stronger and smarter people.

3. People would be unprotected and insecure.

The social compact

John Locke and other philosophers developed a solution to the problems that would exist in a place without government. In a state of nature, people might feel free to do anything they want to do. However, their rights would not be protected and they would feel insecure.

Locke argued that people should agree to give up some of their freedom in exchange for protection and security. They should **consent** to follow laws in exchange for the protection that these laws would give them. This agreement is called a **social compact** or **social contract**. A social compact is an agreement people make among themselves to create a government to rule them and protect their natural rights. In this agreement the people consent to obey the laws created by that government.

In a later lesson, you will study the Declaration of Independence. You will see how the Founders included in the Declaration all the ideas you have studied.

Reviewing and using the lesson

1. What is the purpose of government according to the natural rights philosophers?

2. Where does government get its right to govern, according to the natural rights philosophers?

3. What is a social compact? Do you think this is the best way to create a government? Why or why not?

4. What beliefs about rights were important to the American colonists?

5. What rights do you think people should have?

Before they landed in Plymouth, the Pilgrims signed an agreement called the Mayflower Compact. In it, they each agreed to the formation of a government and to obey its laws. What is such an agreement called?

What is republican government?

Purpose of Lesson

This lesson introduces several more ideas which were important to the Founders when they created our government. When you finish this lesson you should be able to explain these ideas. You should also be able to explain why they were important to the Founders and how they are important to Americans today.

Terms to know

Roman Republic
aristocrats
republican government
common welfare
civic virtue
dictator
separated powers
balanced powers

How could a government that existed over 2,000 years ago influence the development of our Constitution?

The Founders were influenced by their study of history

Over 2,000 years before our nation began, there existed in ancient Europe a government which greatly influenced the ideas of the Founders. This was the **Roman Republic,** which lasted from 509 B.C. to 27 B.C. Its capital was Rome, which was located in what is now called Italy. Some of the ruins of the buildings of this ancient government can still be seen in Rome today.

The Founders were influenced by what historians had written about the people and the government of the Roman Republic. They read that during the Republic, the Roman people governed themselves without a king. The common people and the **aristocrats** (wealthy upper class) shared the power to govern. The people chose leaders to make and administer laws for their country.

The Founders called the government of Rome a **republican government.** They defined a republican government as a type of government in which

- the citizens have the power to govern,

- the citizens give power to leaders they elect to represent them and to serve their interests, and

• the representatives are responsible for promoting the **common welfare** (the good of the entire community).

The Founders thought that republican government was possible in Rome only because of the **civic virtue** of the Roman citizens. Civic virtue meant that both citizens and their leaders lived modest lives. They worked hard and they put the common welfare above their own selfish interests. They believed that the benefits of republican government were that

• the laws made by representatives elected by the people would be fair and would serve the common welfare rather than the selfish interests of one group, and

• people would have greater freedom and be able to live secure and comfortable lives.

The Founders thought a republican form of government was the best form of government they could create for themselves. Then they would have the same benefits they thought the ancient Romans had enjoyed.

Cincinnatus: A model of civic virtue

In the year 460 B.C., Rome was in great danger. An army from the east was burning and plundering the countryside. The defending Roman army was surrounded on all sides by its enemies. The leaders of the government of Rome decided to ask Cincinnatus, a skilled military leader, to help them during this crisis. Messengers were sent asking him to serve as **dictator** (supreme ruler with unlimited power) for as long as the crisis would last.

Cincinnatus was a hard-working farmer with only four acres of land. When the messengers found him, he was quietly plowing the fields. Because he loved his country, he left his plow to go to Rome to lead the army. In a battle that lasted two days, his army defeated the enemy and saved the country. Cincinnatus was honored and praised by his

How did Cincinnatus demonstrate civic virtue?

people. But when the battle was over, he did not try to remain as a dictator of his country. He did not want continued fame. Instead, he returned to his home and his life as a farmer and a citizen.

By returning to his home, Cincinnatus showed that he valued being a citizen of Rome more than he valued fame and personal power. He respected the government of Rome. He did not want to use his popularity to take power away from the representatives elected by the citizens. This was an example of the civic virtue that the Romans were known for during the period of the Republic.

Examining civic virtue

The Founders thought civic virtue was important to make our government work properly. Civic virtue means that people should put the common welfare above their own interests.

The Founders believed that sometimes people might not be willing to give up their own interests. However, they hoped that people would still be kind to others, be willing to help them, and be concerned for their welfare. They thought the family and religion were very important in teaching children to behave in a way that considered the interests of others.

When should you give up your own interests for the common welfare? This is a difficult question that each person has to answer for himself or herself. The following exercise will help you learn how to deal with the question.

Problem solving

Individual interests and the common welfare

Examine the problem of individual interests and the common welfare by discussing such questions as the following. This might be done in groups of about five students. After discussing the questions, a spokesperson for each group should explain its answers to the rest of the class.

1. Describe a person you know or a leader in our nation who you think has civic virtue. Explain what that person did to cause you to think so.

2. Explain some situations in which you think you should put the common welfare above your own interests.

3. Explain some situations in which you might not want to put the common welfare above your own interests.

4. Explain some things a government could do that would be for the common welfare.

5. Explain some situations in which people might disagree about what is best for the common welfare. What should be done when there are such disagreements? Why?

How should a republican government be organized?

The Founders also learned about republican government from Montesquieu (1689-1755). He was a French writer the Founders admired so much that they often called him "the celebrated Montesquieu." They thought he was an expert on what republican government should be like. Montesquieu believed that the best way to

Why was Montesquieu important to the Founders?

make sure a government would serve the common welfare was to do the following things.

- **Separate the powers** of government among the different branches, or parts, of the government so that no one branch would have all the power. Each branch should represent the interests of a different group in society.

- **Balance the powers** among these branches so no one branch would have so much power it could control the others.

- Give each branch ways to **check** the use of power by the other branches.

Montesquieu and many others believed that no single branch could control the entire government if its powers were separated, balanced, and checked. Then no single branch could use the government for its own selfish purposes. The result would be a government that would promote the common welfare.

How were the values of republican government promoted?

The Founders believed the values of republican government were that citizens and their leaders should lead modest lives and work hard. They thought that people should care about the common welfare.

Americans were taught these values in many ways. Parents taught these values to their children. Teachers taught them in school. Ministers taught them in church. Leading citizens of the country were expected to set good examples. These republican values were a part of the customs and traditions of the people.

The ideas and values of the Roman Republic were also promoted throughout America in the stories that people read. People were also reminded of them in the design of public buildings similar to those of ancient Rome.

The Founders thought it was important to teach and promote civic virtue among citizens. They believed that the Roman Republic had failed in the end because its citizens lost their civic virtue. They had promoted their own selfish interests at the expense of the common welfare.

By the time of the American Revolution, the Founders believed strongly in the ideals of republican government. They thought that Great Britain was violating these ideals. They claimed the British government was guilty of serving selfish interests at the expense of the common welfare. It had violated those rights it was the purpose of good government to protect.

After the Revolution, the Founders were able to establish their own government. They tried to make sure this government would not violate their rights. An essential step, they thought, was to create a constitutional government. You will learn what a constitution and a constitutional government are in the next lesson.

Reviewing and using the lesson

1. What is republican government?

2. Why did Montesquieu believe that the powers of republican government should be separated among different branches or groups in the government?

3. What was the purpose of balancing the powers among different groups in the government? Why should each group be given ways to check the power of the other groups?

4. Why was Cincinnatus considered a model of civic virtue?

5. Why do you think many people thought that republican government was not possible if the citizens did not have civic virtue?

6. How was civic virtue promoted among the Founders?

Why do you think religion was so important during the colonial period?

What is constitutional government?

Purpose of Lesson

This lesson introduces three main ideas. They are the ideas of (a) constitution, (b) constitutional government and (c) higher law. Since these ideas are so important in understanding the development of our government, we will define them as clearly as possible. When you finish the lesson you should be able to explain these three ideas. You should also be able to explain some of the important differences between constitutional governments and autocratic or dictatorial governments.

Terms to know

constitution
constitutional government
autocratic or dictatorial government
higher law
private domain

Defining constitution

A **constitution** is a framework for a government. It tells how the government is organized and run. Most constitutions are in writing, such as those of the United States and South Africa. Some are partly written and partly unwritten. The British constitution is the best known example of this kind of constitution. Others are not written at all. Throughout history, most societies had constitutions that were made up of unwritten traditions and customs.

According to this definition of a constitution, every nation has a constitution. Good governments and bad governments have constitutions.

Studying the constitution of a government will help you answer certain questions about that government and its citizens. Here are some of the questions a constitution usually answers:

Questions about the government

- What are the purposes of the government?

- How is the government organized? What parts does it have? What does each part do?

- How is the government supposed to go about doing its business? For example, how are rules made?

- How are people picked to serve in the government?

Questions about citizens

- Who is considered to be a citizen?

- Are citizens supposed to have control over their government? If so, how is this control supposed to work?

- What rights and responsibilities, if any, are the citizens supposed to have?

Defining constitutional government

Having a constitution does not always mean that a nation has a **constitutional government**. A nation has a constitutional government when the powers of the person or group running the government are **limited**. For example, our Constitution limits the powers of the courts. It says they cannot force a person to be a witness against himself or herself.

These limits on the government's power are part of the constitution. In a constitutional government, the people running the government must obey the limits. The constitution contains ways to make sure they obey the limits. Some of the ways constitutions can do this will be described in the next lesson.

As you have learned, all governments have constitutions that set forth the ways they are organized and operated. In some nations, however, power is unlimited. The constitution in such a nation may provide for the unlimited use of power. Or it may say that the power of the government is to be limited without saying how those limitations are to be enforced.

Suppose the constitution of a nation does not limit the powers of its government. Or, suppose it limits the power, but those limits are not enforced. In either situation, the government is not a constitutional government. Such a government of **unlimited power** is called an **autocratic** or **dictatorial** government.

In a constitutional government, the constitution must effectively limit the use of power. The constitution must be considered a **higher law** that has to be obeyed by the people running the government.

Which of these pictures illustrates a country with a constitutional government? Explain your choice.

Defining higher law

In a constitutional government, the constitution or higher law has five important characteristics.

1. It lists the basic rights of citizens to life, liberty, and property.

2. It establishes the responsibility of the government to protect those rights.

3. It places limits on how the people in government can use their powers. Most of these limits are related to three important areas. Examples of how our Constitution limits the powers of government in these areas are the following.

   • **Citizens' rights.** People in our government cannot unfairly deprive us of our right to freedom of speech.

   • **How resources are distributed.** People in our government cannot take a person's property without giving the person fair payment for it.

   • **How conflicts are handled.** People in our government must give persons accused of crime a fair trial.

4. It establishes the principle of a **private domain.** A private domain is an area of an individual's life that is no business of the government. In this area, a person has a right to privacy. For example, the United States government cannot interfere with your right to hold any religious beliefs you might wish to hold.

5. It can only be changed with the widespread consent of the citizens and according to certain set procedures.

Problem solving

Understanding constitutional government

Your class may be divided into five groups. Each group should be assigned one of the five characteristics of constitutional government explained above. Each group should then follow the instructions below. Groups should report their discussions to the rest of the class.

1. Explain the characteristic and give examples. (Students may refer to the copy of the Constitution in this book for ideas.)

2. Explain how important you think this characteristic is.

Note: Students referring to the Constitution will find that it does not contain all the natural rights they have studied. Some are found in the amendments. This will be dealt with in more detail in Unit Five.

Reviewing and using the lesson

1. What is a constitution? What can you learn about a nation's government by studying its constitution?

2. Explain the differences between constitutional governments and autocratic or dictatorial governments.

3. What are the characteristics of the "higher law" of a constitutional government?

4. Describe two areas of citizens' lives with which you think the government should not interfere. Explain why you think the government should not intrude in these areas. What term describes these areas?

How can governments be organized to prevent the abuse of power?

Purpose of Lesson

In the last lesson you learned that a constitutional government is intended to protect the people from abuses of governmental power. This lesson shows some ways in which governments can be organized to make such abuses less likely.

Terms to know

separation of powers
checks and balances
legislative branch
executive branch
judicial branch

Problem solving

The Founders' fear of the abuse of power

The Founders knew that throughout history, many governments had used their power unfairly. They were afraid that the new government they were creating might abuse the powers they gave it. To understand their thinking, read the following quotations from some of the most prominent Founders. Then discuss your answers to the questions that follow.

Give all power to the many, they will oppress the few. Give all power to the few, they will oppress the many. (Alexander Hamilton, American statesman, 1787)

There are two passions which have a powerful influence on the affairs of men. These are ambition and avarice [greed]; the love of power and the love of money. (Benjamin Franklin, American statesman and philosopher, 1787)

From the nature of man, we may be sure that those who have power in their hands . . . will always, when they can . . . increase it. (George Mason, American statesman, 1787)

What view of human nature do these people share? Suppose you agreed with their view. What kinds of protections would you include in your government to prevent it from abusing its powers?

Write a description for this drawing based on the quotes you have just read.

Organizing a constitutional government

You learned in the last lesson that powers are limited in a constitutional government. Constitutional governments are usually organized so one group cannot get enough power to dominate the government. Two ways of organizing government to prevent the abuse of power are called **separation of powers** and **checks and balances**.

Separation of powers

A study of constitutional governments shows that they are often divided into three different groups or branches. All the power of the government is not given to any one branch. Instead, some of the power is given to each branch. For example, in our government we have

- a **legislative branch**, which has the power to make laws,

- an **executive branch**, which has the power to carry out and enforce laws, and

- a **judicial branch**, which has the power to manage conflicts over the interpretation, application, and enforcement of laws.

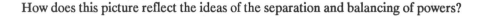

Legislative

Judicial

Executive

How does this picture reflect the ideas of the separation and balancing of powers?

Checks and balances

The phrase **checks and balances** means that powers given to the different branches of government are balanced. No one branch has so much power that it can completely dominate the others. Although each branch of the government has its own special powers, many of these powers are checked because they are shared with the other groups.

In our Constitution, the power to make laws is given to Congress which is the legislative branch of government. This power of Congress is divided between two houses, the House of Representatives and the Senate. Each can check the power of the other by refusing to pass a law proposed by the other house.

In addition, the executive and judicial branches have been given ways to check and control the power of Congress to make laws. For example:

- The President can check the power of Congress. Bills passed by Congress must be signed by the President before they can become laws. The President has the right to **veto** (refuse to sign) a law. If this happens, a bill cannot become a law unless Congress overrides the veto by a vote of two-thirds of the members of both houses.

- The Supreme Court can check the power of Congress. It can declare laws to be in violation of the Constitution and, therefore, invalid.

In much the same way, the powers of the President and Supreme Court are checked. You will learn more about this system of checks and balances in later lessons.

The complications of constitutional government

The complicated system of separated powers and checks and balances helps insure that governmental power is limited. Because constitutional governments are organized in complicated ways, getting things done sometimes takes a long time. It may seem strange, but this is often seen as an advantage. Many people think that these complications make it more likely that when a decision is finally made, it will be a good one.

Reviewing and using the lesson

1. What branches do many modern constitutional governments have? What are the functions of each branch?

2. Why are powers divided among separate groups?

3. In constitutional governments, one branch is often checked by the other branches. Why? Give examples of some checks.

4. The separation and sharing of powers means that decisions are not made quickly. Explain at least one way this could be an advantage. Then, explain at least one way it could be a disadvantage.

Unit Two: What experiences shaped the Founders' thinking about government?

The first legislative assembly in America met in Virginia in 1619.
Why was representative government important to the colonists?

Purpose of Unit Two

In the last unit, you learned some important ideas and questions about government. You studied the natural rights philosophy, republicanism, and constitutionalism. These were the ideas that influenced the Founders of our nation and helped shape their views about government.

In this unit, you will learn more about the Founders and Framers. You will learn how they and other Americans lived. You will read about the experiences that shaped their thinking about government. You will study their values and the things they believed were important. You will also learn why they thought a new constitution was necessary. This unit will finish setting the stage for studying about the actual writing of our Constitution.

Throughout this book, we will sometimes talk about England and other times refer to Great Britain. In 1707, England and Scotland (which until then had its own Parliament) joined with Wales to create the kingdom of Great Britain. Therefore, when we speak of events occurring after 1707, we will refer to England as Great Britain.

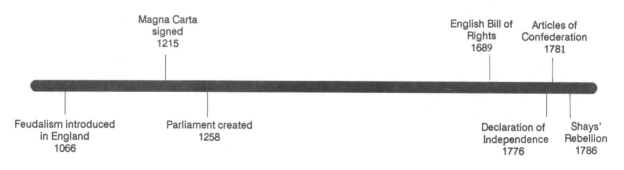

Magna Carta
signed
1215

English Bill of
Rights
1689

Articles of
Confederation
1781

Feudalism introduced
in England
1066

Parliament created
1258

Declaration of
Independence
1776

Shays'
Rebellion
1786

How were the Americans influenced by their English background?

Purpose of Lesson

This lesson describes the growth and development of constitutional government in England. It discusses the limitations that were placed on that government over a period of many centuries. It will help you to understand the background of the basic ideas of constitutional government in the American colonies.

When you have finished this lesson, you should be able to describe the struggles for power between the English monarch (king or queen) and the Parliament (legislature). You should also be able to explain how these struggles led to a system of separated powers and representative government.

Terms to know
feudalism/feudal system
royalty
monarch/monarchy
nobility
common people
Magna Carta
representative government
Parliament
English Bill of Rights

Americans' knowledge of British government

The American colonies had been ruled by the British government for over 150 years before the American Revolution. As a result, Americans knew quite a bit about the British government. The men who wrote our Constitution were greatly influenced by their experiences with the British government. They were also influenced by their knowledge of its history. Understanding what they knew is important to understanding why they wrote the Constitution as they did.

The feudal system

English history goes back many centuries before the discovery of America. For much of that time, England was made up of a number of kingdoms, each with its own ruler. Then, in 1066, William the Conqueror invaded England and became its king. He then began a new system of government known as **feudalism**.

Under the **feudal system**, the people in England belonged to one of the following three groups.

- **Royalty.** This group included the **monarch** (king or queen) and his or her family. A government ruled by a monarch is called a **monarchy**.

- **Nobility**. This group included the "lords" and "ladies" who held titles such as earl, duke, duchess, and baron. They worked for the king and made it possible for him to control all of England.

- **Common people**. The group included such people as knights (soldiers of the king), merchants, and peasants (people who worked the land). The peasants were often called serfs because they were not free and could not leave the area in which they worked.

England's land all belonged to the king or queen. There was too much land for a king or queen to rule alone. So, they gave some of the responsibility for governing the kingdom to the nobility. Under the feudal system, the nobles were allowed to control parts of the land and the people who lived there. In exchange, they pledged their loyalty to the king and fought for him. You will see how this sharing of power by royalty with the nobility eventually led to a government that represented more of the people.

How does this drawing illustrate the distribution of power in the feudal system?

What changes occurred in the distribution of power when the Magna Carta was signed?

The Magna Carta

Under the feudal system, it became a custom or tradition for the royalty to share some of its powers with the nobility. As a result, the nobles became used to having certain rights and powers. When King John tried to take back some of these rights, the nobles rebelled.

The nobles were powerful enough to force the king to sign an agreement with them. This agreement, signed by King John in 1215, became known as the **Magna Carta** or Great Charter. It said that the nobles would obey the king only as long as he protected their rights.

The Magna Carta was a major step in the growth of English constitutional government. It contained two very important ideas:

- Governments are based on an agreement or contract between the ruler and people to be ruled. In the case of the Magna Carta, this was a contract between the king and the nobility.

Most of the people in England were not a part of this agreement. But it was an early step in establishing the idea that government should be based on a contract which includes all the people. You may recognize this as the same idea as the social contract discussed hundreds of years later by the natural rights philosophers.

A government by contract means that both sides of the agreement are responsible for fulfilling its terms. In the Magna Carta, the king was responsible for not depriving the nobility of their rights. The nobility, in turn, was responsible for supporting the king and obeying the laws of England.

A government by contract also includes the idea that if either side breaks the contract it is no longer valid.

- The Magna Carta also includes the idea of the rule of law. This means that both the government and the governed must obey the law. The law limits the powers of the government. For example, the king could not take away the property of a noble without following agreed-upon procedures and rules.

The rule of law also meant that if the king broke the laws, the nobles had the right to overthrow him. They could place a new king on the throne. This idea became part of the natural rights philosophy. It is also included in our Declaration of Independence.

The early English customs and traditions and the Magna Carta protected certain basic rights. These rights were not given to all the people of England. Men who owned property were given far more rights than other people. Men without property, and women and children had fewer rights. However, the Magna Carta was an important step in protecting the rights of the people and limiting the power of the government.

The establishment of Parliament

Important changes in the English government resulted in the establishment of other basic ideas you have studied. These are the separation of powers and the beginnings of **representative government**. In 1258, the nobles forced King Henry III to create a new council called **Parliament** to advise the monarch. Parliament was made up of two houses which represented the most powerful groups in the kingdom. The House of Lords represented the nobles. The House of Commons represented people who owned large amounts of land but were not members of the nobility.

For hundreds of years after the creation of Parliament, the royalty, nobility, and commons struggled for power. No one group was able to control all the power for very long. The struggle became so intense during the 17th century that a civil war resulted. The nobles won and in 1649, Parliament ordered the execution of the king. By the time of the Glorious Revolution of

Who benefited most from the creation of Parliament?

1688, the balance of power had shifted in favor of Parliament.

The English Bill of Rights

In 1689, Parliament passed an important law, the **English Bill of Rights**. This law gave certain rights to Englishmen and further limited the powers of the monarch. The Bill of Rights gave Parliament the balance of power in the English government.

What did the Bill of Rights guarantee? It said that elections to Parliament must be free and that the people have the right to keep and carry weapons. It said that kings and queens were not allowed to

- collect taxes without the consent of Parliament,

- interfere with the right to free speech and debate that went on in Parliament,

- maintain an army in times of peace (since it might be used to take over the government),

- require excessive bail or administer cruel punishment for those accused or convicted of crimes,

- declare that laws made by Parliament should not be obeyed.

By the end of the 17th century, the British government became increasingly limited in what it could do. During this same period, the government was establishing colonies in North America. The colonists brought with them the English system of constitutional government.

Problem solving

Your class should be divided into small groups to answer the following questions. When your group has completed its answers, it should share them with the rest of the class.

The Magna Carta was written in 1215 and the English Bill of Rights was passed in 1689. During the more than 400 years between these documents, many changes occurred in the English government. Review what you have read about these two documents and discuss the following questions.

1. How was the Bill of Rights different from the Magna Carta?

2. What basic rights that you think are important were not included in either of these two documents?

Reviewing and using the lesson

1. How and why did the feudal kings in England share their power?

2. What were some of the basic ideas included in the Magna Carta?

3. Parliament won a struggle with the king in 1689, when the English Bill of Rights was adopted. Which parts of the English Bill of Rights do you think the Framers might have included in our Constitution? Explain your answers.

4. Four ideas that were very important to the Framers were limited government, representative government, the balance of power, and separation of powers. Give examples of these ideas from English government.

What experiences led to the American Revolution?

Purpose of Lesson

In the last lesson, you learned about the growth of constitutional government in England. Great Britain ruled the American colonies for more than 150 years. This lesson will help you understand how British ideas of constitutional government were used in the colonial governments. You will also learn why the colonists came to feel that the British government threatened their rights.

When you have finished this lesson, you should be able to explain how constitutional government developed in the colonies. You should also be able to explain some of the reasons the American colonists decided to fight for their independence.

Terms to know
colonial government
indentured servant
governor
magistrate
Continental Congress
Loyalists

Constitutional government in the colonies

The colonists who came to America from England thought of themselves as loyal subjects of England. They brought with them English customs, English laws, and English ideas about good government. They modeled their **colonial governments** after what they knew of the English system.

Each of the thirteen English colonies had its own government. All thirteen, however, contained the following basic ideas of English constitutional government.

1. Natural rights — Colonial governments were based on the idea that the purpose of government is to protect the people's natural rights to life, liberty, and property.

Many rights, however, were only given to white men who owned a certain amount of property. People who usually did not have such rights were women, free white men who did not own property, **indentured servants** (people who had to work for a master for a specific time), free black men, slaves, and Native Americans.

2. Higher law — English law was considered a higher law. It was superior to any laws the colonial governments made. Colonial governments could not do anything that violated the English constitution. After 1689, this meant that colonial legislatures were under the rule of Parliament.

3. Separation of powers — As in England, the powers of the colonial governments were separated among three branches. This system was designed to protect the people from the abuse of power.

- The executive branch was headed by a **governor** who carried out and enforced the law. Governors in most of the colonies were chosen by the king or the owners of the colony.

- The legislative branch made the laws. Most colonies had legislatures with two houses, like the English Parliament.

- The judicial branch was made up of judges or **magistrates**. They were usually appointed by the governor. Their responsibility was to handle conflicts over the laws. They presided at the trials of people accused of breaking the law. They also made sure that colonial laws did not violate the higher law of England.

4. Checks and balances — Power in some cases was shared among the branches. Use of power by one branch could be checked by that of another. For example, the governors could not collect taxes without the consent of the legislature. The legislature was checked by the magistrates who made sure that the laws did not violate those of England. The powers of the magistrates were checked because they had to rely on the governor to enforce their decisions.

5. Representative government and the right to vote — Government that contained representatives of the people began soon after the first colonies were established. The first representative assembly was held in Virginia in 1619. After the English Bill of Rights was passed in 1689, Parliament said that at least one house in each colony's legislature had to be elected by eligible voters.

The British government tightens control over the colonies

For much of the colonial period, Great Britain paid little attention to the colonies. Britain had become a world power and was often busy with European wars. In addition, the colonies were a long way from England and communication was slow. As a result, the colonists became used to governing themselves. However, by the mid-18th century the British government began to show a new interest in America.

New World   Atlantic Ocean   Old World

What does this picture illustrate about British control over the American colonies?

The colonies were seen as a source of money from taxes and trade.

During the years of British neglect, the American colonists had been able to disobey trade laws made by Parliament. However, the situation changed after Britain ended its war with France in 1763. Although victorious, the British were left a national debt that had doubled in size. To reduce that debt, Parliament raised taxes in both Britain and America. The British government also began to tighten trade regulations. The colonists were asked to bear their share of running the empire.

The colonists viewed the new laws differently than did the government in Great Britain. In the years from 1763 to 1774, the actions of Parliament convinced many Americans their rights were being threatened. Some colonists began to think about breaking away from Great Britain. As John Adams wrote Thomas Jefferson, "the Revolution was in the minds of the people from...1760 to 1775...before a drop of blood was shed at Lexington."

British actions that led to the Revolution included:

- **Proclamation Line** (1763). This act forbade Americans to settle in certain western lands.

- **Stamp Act** (1765). This act taxed every legal document, newspaper, pamphlet, deck of cards, and dice.

- **Quartering Act** (1765). This act required colonists to allow British soldiers to stay in their homes.

- **Declaratory Act** (1766). This act stated Parliament had the right to pass laws for the colonies in "all cases whatsoever."

- **Boston Massacre** (1770). British troops opened fire at a crowd of colonists and killed five Americans.

- **Tea Act** (1773). In what became known as the Boston Tea Party, colonists threw British tea into Boston harbor to show their dissatisfaction with the unfairness of the tea taxes.

How do you think the colonists reacted when Britain tightened its control?

- **Intolerable Acts** (1774). This act limited local government in Massachusetts and closed the Boston harbor.

While the colonists thought their rights were threatened, most British citizens felt the Americans were behaving like ungrateful children. They believed that the prosperity and security of the Americans were due to the help they received from the British government. It was only fair that they share part of the burden of government. The colonial concern with representation in Parliament made little sense to most Englishmen. Parliament did not represent individuals or geographical areas. Instead, it was thought to represent the interests of the whole nation no matter where its members lived.

The colonists begin to resist

The colonists believed that their rights would be protected only when their interests were represented in the government. The colonists did not have the right to vote for representatives in Parliament. Therefore they claimed that Parliament had no right to tax them. Their rallying cry was "no taxation without representation."

There were an increasing number of conflicts with the British government. By the fall of 1774 these conflicts had led many colonists to decide it was time to take united action. Twelve of the thirteen colonies sent representatives to a meeting in Philadelphia. This meeting was the First **Continental Congress**. It was the start of a unified American government.

On April 19, 1775, war broke out between Great Britain and her American colonies. On that day, British troops marched to Concord, Massachusetts, to capture the arms and ammunition hidden there by the colonists. The British soldiers hoped to surprise the Americans, but the colonists had been warned. In the towns of Lexington and Concord, the first shots of the American Revolution were fired.

What was the result of colonial resistance?

A few weeks later, representatives of the colonies met in Philadelphia for the Second Continental Congress. The Congress decided to resist the British. It called upon the colonies to raise troops for the Continental army to be led by George Washington. A year later, Congress asked a committee to draft a document explaining why the colonists felt it was necessary to free themselves from British rule. This document is known as the Declaration of Independence.

Problem solving

There were strong differences of opinion between Americans who supported the revolutionary cause and those who supported the British position. To better understand these differences, the class should be divided into four groups, two supporting the revolutionary cause and two opposing it. After each group has presented its position, the class should decide which group—the supporters or opponents of the Revolution—has the stronger position.

1. Supporters of the Revolution (Patriots)

- Group one should write a letter to the editor of a colonial newspaper defending the actions of the Second Continental Congress in opposing the British.

- Group two should draw an editorial cartoon defending the American position in the conflict with Great Britain.

2. Supporters of the British position (Loyalists)

- Group three should write a letter to the editor of a colonial newspaper explaining why the British actions were justified.

- Group four should draw an editorial cartoon supporting those who remained faithful to Great Britain.

Reviewing and using the lesson

1. Colonial governments illustrated English ideas of good government. Describe the similarities between the colonial governments and the English government.

2. For most of the colonial period, the colonists considered themselves to be loyal subjects of Great Britain. Why do you think they felt this way? What happened to change the feelings of many colonists?

3. The colonists believed that one of the main purposes of government was to protect the individual's property rights. This was an important reason why they limited the right to vote to those men who owned property. What arguments can you give to support this policy? What arguments would you use to oppose this policy?

What basic ideas about government were in the Declaration of Independence?

Purpose of Lesson

One of the most important documents in American history is the Declaration of Independence. It summarizes the colonists' basic ideas about government. It also lists their complaints against the British king and justifies their decision to declare independence. When you have finished this lesson, you should be able to explain the main ideas contained in the Declaration.

Terms to know
unalienable rights
consent of the governed

How did Jefferson justify the colonists' revolt against Great Britain?

Writing the Declaration

Thomas Jefferson was a man of many talents. He was a statesman, a diplomat, an author, an architect, and a scientist. Born in Virginia, Jefferson was a member of the Continental Congress during the Revolutionary War. He was a quiet, shy man, not known as a great speaker. He worked well, however, in small committees. Members of Congress admired his excellent writing style and chose him to draft the Declaration of Independence.

Jefferson spent many evenings writing and revising the Declaration. He showed the draft to the other members of the committee: Benjamin Franklin of Pennsylvania, John Adams of Massachusetts, Roger Sherman of Connecticut, and Robert R. Livingston of New York. They suggested changes, as did the Continental Congress. On July 4, 1776, the Declaration was signed by the members of Congress.

The contents of the Declaration

The Declaration was an important statement in the development of our constitutional government. It is also an excellent example of the arguments of the natural rights philosophy. The Declaration was written to justify the American Revolution against the British. It contains several important parts.

- **Ideals**. It is one of the best statements of the ideals of our nation.

- **Arguments**. It gives the reasons why the colonists thought they were justified in breaking away from Great Britain.

- **Complaints**. It lists the complaints of the colonists against the king.

- **Conclusion**. "...That these United Colonies are, and of Right ought to be, Free and Independent States;..."

Ideals of the Declaration

The Declaration of Independence sets forth some of the most important ideals of our constitutional democracy. It states that all men are created equal and that they all have certain basic rights. These are the rights to life, liberty, and the pursuit of happiness. Throughout our history, many people have worked hard to make these ideals a reality for everyone.

Part of the Declaration is printed below. Some of the words used may be new to you. The meanings of these words are given in brackets after the words. As you read it, compare the ideas it contains with the ideas of the natural rights philosophy you have studied.

We hold these Truths to be self-evident [easy for anyone to see], that all Men are created equal, that they are endowed [given] by their Creator [God] with certain unalienable Rights [basic or natural rights that cannot be taken away], that among these are Life, Liberty, and the Pursuit of Happiness — That to secure these Rights, Governments are instituted [established] among Men, deriving [receiving] their just Powers from the Consent [agreement] of the Governed, that whenever any Form of Government becomes destructive of these Ends [purposes], it is the Right of the People to alter or to abolish it, and to institute new Government...

What ideas were included in the Declaration of Independence?

Arguments of the Declaration

The Declaration was a justification for the American Revolution. Jefferson used the ideas of the natural rights philosophy in this argument. The main points of the argument are listed below. See if you can identify its relationship to the natural rights philosophy.

1. The rights of the people are based on natural law. Natural law is a higher law than laws made by people. (Many of the Founders believed natural law came from God.) Neither constitutions nor governments may violate the natural law. The only rightful purpose of government is to protect the people's natural rights.

2. If a government violates the natural law, the people have the right to change or abolish the government and form a new one.

3. An agreement existed between the colonists and the king. The colonists consented to be governed by the king so long as he protected their rights to life, liberty, and property.

4. No agreement had been made between the colonists and Parliament. So Parliament had no right to govern the colonies or to tax them. This was especially true, argued the colonists, since they did not have the right to send representatives to Parliament.

5. The king had violated his agreement with the colonists by acting with Parliament to deprive them of their rights. Therefore, the colonists had the right to withdraw their consent to be governed by the king. They were free to establish their own government.

Complaints against the King

The Declaration contains a long list of complaints against the British king. The complete text of the Declaration is included at the end of this book. The following activity will help you understand these complaints.

Problem solving

Basic ideas underlying the complaints of the Declaration

Your class should be divided into small groups. Each group should examine the text of the Declaration of Independence and select three complaints against the king. Each group should then complete the following exercise and report its findings to the rest of the class.

- Rewrite the complaint in your own words.

- Explain the basis of the colonists' complaint.

Reviewing and using the lesson

1. What was the purpose of the Declaration of Independence?

2. What is the purpose of government as described in the Declaration of Independence? How is this purpose similar to or different from the purpose of government described by the natural rights philosophers?

3. What does the Declaration say people have a right to do if a government is destructive of their rights? Is this true today? Why or why not?

4. What do you think was meant by the phrase "all men are created equal"? In 1776, who was included? Who was not?

How did the states govern themselves after the Revolution?

Purpose of Lesson

Even before the signing of the Declaration of Independence in 1776, the former colonies were establishing state governments. Many had begun to write new constitutions for their states shortly after the Revolutionary War started in 1775.

Never before had so many new governments been created using the basic ideas of natural rights, republican government, and constitutional government. In this lesson you will look at the state governments and the basic ideas upon which they were founded. When you complete the lesson you should be able to describe those basic ideas. You should also be able to explain the major differences between the Massachusetts constitution and the constitutions of the other states.

Terms to know

popular sovereignty
legislative supremacy
faction

Writing the state constitutions

The Founders wanted to create state governments that would protect the basic rights of the people and promote the common welfare. When they began to write their state constitutions they remembered and used the ideas they had learned from political philosophy. They also used what they had learned from their own experiences with colonial and British government.

The ideas the Founders included in the state constitutions were not new. Most of them had been used in the governments of the colonies. The Founders tried to design their new governments with the best ideas from the past. Their experiences with these state governments would help the Framers design the Constitution in 1787. The basic ideas included in the state constitutions are described below.

Basic ideas in the state constitutions

1. **Natural rights and higher law.** The purpose of government was to protect the rights of citizens to life, liberty, and property. Each state constitution was considered to be a higher law that everyone in the government had to obey.

2. **Social contract.** The people agreed to form a government to protect their natural rights. This agreement was the social contract among the people.

3. **Popular sovereignty.** All the state constitutions contained the idea that the people are the source of the authority of the government. Government gets its right to govern from the people.

4. **Representation**. Each state considered it very important that the legislature be made up of elected representatives of the people. In most states the right to vote was limited to white men who owned property. However, about 70% of the white men in America owned enough property to be able to vote. In contrast, only about 10% of the men were eligible to vote in Great Britain.

The basic ideas of natural rights, social contract, popular sovereignty, and representation had all been part of the colonial governments. These were ideas that the colonists had brought with them from Great Britain. There were, however, some important differences between the colonial governments and those set up by most of the states after 1775.

Problem solving

How was power balanced by the state constitutions?

Look at the two illustrations on this page and answer the questions that follow. Share your answers with the rest of your class.

- How was power balanced in most states?

- Compare the balance of power in Massachusetts with the balance of power in the other states.

- What do you think might be the advantages and disadvantages of giving most of the power of a government to the legislature?

- What do you think might be the advantages and disadvantages of the system of government in Massaschusetts?

What differences in the balance of power are shown in these drawings?

Legislative supremacy

The majority of the states set up governments in which most of the power was given to the legislature. This system of government is known as **legislative supremacy**. The Founders believed that because the legislature was elected by the people, it was the most democratic branch of government. They were afraid of giving too much power to the executive. They remembered how the royal governors and the king had abused their power. So most of the state governors were given very limited power.

There were some checks on the power of the legislative branch. Most states had two houses in the legislature, each of which could check the power of the other. However, the legislature had far greater power than the other two branches of the government.

Legislative supremacy led to serious problems in most states

- State governments did not protect the property rights of some citizens. In these states, factions—groups of people who seek to promote their own interests—gained control of the legislature. The factions were accused of making laws that benefited themselves rather than the common welfare. For example, they passed laws which canceled debts and created paper money. These laws benefited the people who owed money and hurt those who had loaned it to them.

- The state legislatures passed laws that taxed and controlled their citizens far more than the British had done. The level of taxes during the 1780s was ten to twenty times what it had been before the Revolution.

- Many new state laws were passed which interfered with the private lives of the citizens. Laws were passed telling people what they should eat, drink, wear, and believe.

The Massachusetts constitution

In 1780, Massachusetts became the last state to ratify (approve) its constitution. The citizens there had learned some important lessons from the experiences of the other states. They used this knowledge in creating their government. It is worth seeing what was different about this constitution.

The people of Massachusetts felt that three things were necessary to protect the rights of the people.

- Representation

- Separation of powers

- Checks and balances

Most of the other states relied on a system of legislative supremacy to protect people's rights. The Massachusetts constitution distributed power more evenly among the different branches of government. The governor was given more power and was more independent of the legislature than in other states. Because the people elected him directly, they expected him to protect their interests. Some of the powers of the governor of Massachusetts are described on the next page. You can see how the powers of the governor were balanced in relation to the legislature.

- The governor was given a fixed salary which could not be changed by the legislature.

- He could veto laws made by the legislature and his veto could only be over-ridden by a two-thirds vote of the legislature.

- The governor was given the power to appoint officials in the executive branch and judges in the judicial branch.

The Massachusetts constitution divided the people into voting groups based on their wealth. They expected that government would then more accurately represent the interests of all the people.

- Only people with a large amount of property could vote for the governor and the legislature.

- People with slightly less property could vote for the upper and lower houses of the legislature.

- Eligible voters with the minimum amount of property could vote for the lower house of the legislature.

The experience of writing state constitutions was a useful one. Americans were learning about what type of government worked best. The differences between the Massachusetts constitution and those that were written earlier were a result of these experiences.

Reviewing and using the lesson

1. Why did most of the state constitutions give most of the power to the legislature?

2. The Massachusetts constitution differed in important ways from those of the other states. Describe these differences.

3. Explain what you think might be the advantages and disadvantages of the Massachusetts constitution compared with the constitutions of the other states.

4. Do you think the property requirements for voting were in conflict with the principles of democracy? Explain your answer.

What were Americans like in the 1780s?

Purpose of Lesson

Americans in the 1780s were in some ways similar but in other ways quite different from the Europeans of the time. Although Americans had brought many British customs with them, they had begun to develop their own way of life. This lesson should help you understand how most Americans lived two hundred years ago. It should also help you understand some of the differences between the ways people lived in America and in Europe.

Terms to know

self-sufficient
literate

Geography and population

In 1787 the United States was not as large as it is today. It was, however, a very large country compared with most of the nations of Europe. For example, England was only slightly larger than the state of New York. The settled area of the United States stretched twelve hundred miles along the coast of the Atlantic Ocean and ran two hundred miles inland. Between this settled coastal area and the Mississippi River lay a great area of forested land which few white men had explored.

Although the land was large, there were very few people living in the nation. In 1790, the country's population was almost 4 million people compared with over 240 million today. The average number of people living in each square mile of land at that time was 4.5. Today there are 60 people per square mile.

Most people did not live in cities. They lived on farms or in small communities or villages. New York and Philadelphia were the only two cities in the entire country that had over 25,000 people living in them.

Ninety percent of white Americans were farmers. A typical farm was between 90 and 160 acres. Farms varied from the small 30-acre plot of the poorest New England farmers to giant southern plantations with thousands of acres.

People lived quite differently from one region of the nation to the next. For example, people in the small farms and villages of Massachusetts lived very differently from people living on the slave-holding plantations of South Carolina.

A self-sufficient people

Since most people lived far from each other, they had to develop the knowledge and skills to provide for themselves. The people became very **self-sufficient**, that is, they took care of themselves rather than depending upon others for most of their needs. For example, not only did they raise their own food, but they wove cloth to make their own clothes. They made their own medicines, built their homes and barns, and made their furniture and tools. They took the surplus produce from their farms and traded it for goods they could not make.

Americans traded among themselves and they helped each other. Barns would be built by neighbors working together. But usually Americans lived fairly isolated lives. Families worked on their own. Rarely would they travel more than fifty miles from their homes. On the frontier, farm families often lived 10 miles from their nearest neighbor.

Farm families frequently included a hired man or an indentured servant. In the South, farm families often had slaves. Not all white Americans were independent farmers. Some were hired laborers or craftsmen working on large farms. Another small but important group lived in villages and cities and worked in professions, trades, crafts, and factories.

The typical white family of the time had the highest standard of living in the world. People worked hard, but the land was fertile and crops grew well. As a result, they ate well, with diets rich in protein. Consequently, Americans tended to be healthier and taller than Europeans.

Not only did average white Americans live better than most Europeans, they were better educated. In fact, more American citizens were **literate**—able to read and write—than in any other nation on earth. The most popular publications, other than the Bible, were newspapers. Newspapers were so popular there were four times as many published in the United States as in France, which was the most literate nation in Europe.

What are some examples of self-sufficiency that you see in this picture?

Southern plantations depended on slave labor. How would life there be different from life in a northern city?

Although most white Americans lived fairly well, this was not true of everyone. One-fifth of the population was black, and most blacks were slaves. Nearly all the slaves lived in the South and worked on large farms or plantations. Slaves were often treated harshly. Even free blacks in the North suffered from discrimination.

Differences in background

Most people in the United States spoke English, belonged to Protestant churches, and were descended from British or Irish settlers. However, not all of the people were from English-speaking countries. Settlers came from Germany, Sweden, France, the Netherlands, Spain, and other countries, bringing with them their own customs. Blacks were taken as slaves from many African societies. Many Native Americans also lived within the borders of the new nation.

There were important differences in people's religious beliefs. Although most Americans were Protestants, there were many different sects, or groups, of Protestants. And some of the immigrants were Catholics and Jews. Compared to a European nation of the time, the United States was very diverse indeed.

Class differences

Most people lived well in the United States. The nation was not divided into a few rich people and a large mass of poor people as in most of Europe. There was no royalty and no titled nobility in America.

People thought of American society as being divided into different social ranks, or classes. The "gentlemen" or "well-born" people were considered to be of a higher rank. These were often the large land-owners, merchants, lawyers, and ministers. The average people were the lower rank — the "common sort." The common people tended to choose the rich and well-born to represent them in government.

As a result of this distinction, the upper class was often given the power to make decisions for the community. Over the years, however, the difference between the gentlemen and the common sort became less important. The common man could become wealthy by using his knowledge, skills, and the opportunities provided him. He could also be elected to a government position.

Limits on opportunities

Not all people shared the same opportunities to gain wealth or to become leaders. Usually, only adult white males who owned property could vote. Native Americans, blacks, white men who owned no property, and women were typically not allowed to vote or hold office. Women usually were not allowed to own property. Under the law, a married woman was considered to be one person with her husband and he controlled the property.

Attitudes towards government

Since most Americans were so self-sufficient, they valued their freedom highly. They felt superior to the corrupt societies of Europe and thought of themselves as virtuous, God-fearing, hard-working, plain-living people. They had just defeated the most powerful army on earth.

In the years following the Revolution, Americans were very sensitive to any attempts to limit their freedom. They were concerned with protecting the rights they had just won.

Reviewing and using the lesson

1. What was the most common occupation in America in 1787? What kind of standard of living did it provide? What attitudes did it create?

2. What differences of race and wealth were there in American society? How do these differences compare with America today?

3. Do you think the diversity of Americans increased their acceptance of people with different beliefs and life-styles? Why or why not?

How do you think the lives of city people differed from those of farmers?

Why did the Founders think a new constitution was needed?

Purpose of Lesson

After declaring independence in 1776, the Continental Congress formed a committee to write a plan of government for the country. The result of that committee's work was our first national constitution, the Articles of Confederation. It was not easy to create a government that the states could agree on. It took five years before every state ratified the new constitution.

Under the Articles of Confederation, the national government successfully conducted the war against Britain and accomplished some important tasks. Despite its successes, however, there were serious problems with the Articles of Confederation.

When you have completed this lesson you should be able to describe the creation of the Articles of Confederation. You should also be able to explain how the problems with the Articles of Confederation caused the Founders to write a new constitution.

Terms to know

national government
Confederation Congress
Articles of Confederation
Northwest Ordinance
Shays' Rebellion

The creation of the Articles of Confederation

It was not easy to write and agree upon a new constitution for the United States. The Founders had to deal with a number of difficult questions. What type of **national government** should they create? How much power should they give it?

Many people feared giving too much power to a central government because of their experience under British rule. Another fear was that some states might have so much power in the national government that they could dominate the others. Both of these fears influenced the organization of the first American government.

The result was that the Founders created a weak national government. Each state had one vote no matter how large its population. The legislature, called the **Confederation Congress**, had only one house. There was no executive branch to carry out the laws passed by Congress. Instead, the country was run by congressional committees, causing much confusion.

The states were afraid that Congress might be able to control them. So they made sure that Congress was weak and its powers limited. The states kept most of the power. Every action taken by Congress had to be with the consent, approval, and cooperation of the states. Nine of the thirteen states had to approve any decision

Congress made in order for it to become law. All thirteen had to agree to any change in the Articles of Confederation.

Achievements under the Articles of Confederation

The national government under the Articles of Confederation was responsible for a number of important achievements.

- It successfully waged the war for independence against Great Britain.

- It negotiated a peace treaty, the Treaty of Paris, to end the American Revolution.

- It provided that each state recognize the laws of the other states. A marriage in one state would be valid in all other states. A citizen could travel freely from one state to another. Criminals who had crossed state borders could be sent back to the state in which they committed their crime.

- It passed the **Northwest Ordinance** of 1787. This was the most important law passed by Congress under the Articles. It gave people in the northwestern lands the right to organize their own governments. Once they had done this, they could ask to be admitted as new states with the same rights as the original thirteen states. The law also provided for public education and forbade slavery. The western settlers were guaranteed freedom of worship, the right to trial by jury, and due process of law.

These were major accomplishments. However, there were serious problems with the national government that led to the decision to develop a new constitution.

Problems under the Articles of Confederation

- Congress had no money and no power to get it. It had to rely upon voluntary contributions from the state governments. This system did not work because the states argued about their fair shares of governmental expenses. Some states refused to pay what they had agreed to pay. The national government could not do anything about this.

- Congress had no power over the state governments and their citizens. If individual citizens or a state government ignored a resolution passed by Congress, there was no way to make them obey.

- Congress could not make the states live up to trade agreements with other nations. Sometimes citizens refused to pay for goods they purchased from abroad. This made people in foreign countries unwilling to trade with the United States.

- Congress failed to protect American citizens from unfair discrimination by the states. Americans who had supported the British during the Revolution faced many hardships. States refused to pay for property that had been taken from the Loyalists. Debts owed to Loyalists from before the

Revolution were not honored after the war.

- Congress had no power to prevent unfair competition among the states. States taxed goods from other states and trading often became impossible. Business slowed down and people lost their jobs.

People who were being hurt by these actions argued that the state governments were not protecting their property. They believed all states should use the same money. They thought that legal agreements made in one state should be honored throughout the nation. Many of these people began to think that a strong national government was needed to protect their property rights.

How does this picture illustrate the problems of Congress under the Articles of Confederation?

Shays' Rebellion

By 1786, ten years after the Declaration of Independence, many Americans were in a difficult financial situation. Businesses failed, trade suffered, and many people were in debt. Soldiers who had fought in the Revolution still had not been paid. Congress could not control the country and people worried about what would happen. A dramatic event occurred that finally convinced many Americans it was time for a change.

Farmers in Massachusetts had serious economic problems. Farm prices were low, and when farmers could not pay their debts, many lost their farms and homes. Some were even put in prison. Many people claimed that the new state taxes had put them in debt. As a result, they felt that the state was not protecting their interests.

Farmers began to close down local courts to keep the state from taking their farms. These closures spread to other counties and into neighboring states. In November, 1786, several hundred angry farmers in Massachusetts gathered under the leadership of Daniel Shays. They needed weapons to use in their rebellion against the state government. Shays' followers tried to capture the arsenal at Springfield where arms were kept for the state militia.

Although Shays' followers were defeated, Shays' Rebellion frightened many property owners. They feared that such actions might become widespread. The national government had not been able to put down the rebellion because it had no troops. People were asking how the country could continue to exist if it could not keep law and order.

Shays' Rebellion and the difficulties of governing under the Articles of Confederation led to the call for a new constitution. This was not an easy decision nor was it done quickly. In 1786 Virginia invited all the states to send representatives to a meeting in Annapolis, Maryland. The purpose was to consider trade problems. Only five states sent representatives.

The Annapolis meeting sent a report to the Confederation Congress requesting a convention of all the states to revise the Articles. After much deliberation, Congress invited the states to send delegates to a convention in Philadelphia. This convention would be "for the sole and express purpose of revising the Articles of Confederation."

Why did Shays' Rebellion frighten many Americans?

43

Problem solving

Was a new constitution needed?

As states prepared to select delegates for the Philadelphia Convention, they had to decide what position their delegates would take. To better understand the issues involved, your class should be divided into four groups. Each group should take one of the positions below. Groups may wish to review the above sections on the creation, achievements, and problems of the government under the Articles in developing their positions.

- Defend the Articles of Confederation as the best way to organize the national government.

- Argue that the Articles should be kept, but revised to make up for their weaknesses. Explain the proposed revisions.

- Argue to scrap the Articles and write a new constitution.

- Listen to the arguments presented by the other three groups and decide the position of your state's delegates at the Philadelphia Convention.

Reviewing and using the lesson

1. Why might people from states with smaller populations have been satisfied with the government set up by the Articles of Confederation?

2. Why do you think some people today still oppose a strong national government? Name some issues that states might prefer to decide for themselves.

Unit Three: What happened at the Philadelphia Convention?

How was our Constitution written?

Purpose of Unit Three

You now are familiar with the knowledge and experiences of the Founders of our government. This unit will help you understand why the Framers wrote the Constitution as they did. You will study some of the major problems facing the Framers and how they solved them.

When you have completed this unit, you should be able to explain how the Constitution was written. You should also be able to describe some of the disagreements that occurred during the Philadelphia Convention and how the Framers compromised these differences. Finally, you should be able to explain the positions of the Founders who supported the Constitution and those who were against it.

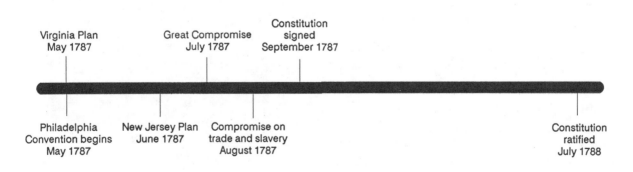

Virginia Plan
May 1787

Great Compromise
July 1787

Constitution
signed
September 1787

Philadelphia
Convention begins
May 1787

New Jersey Plan
June 1787

Compromise on
trade and slavery
August 1787

Constitution
ratified
July 1788

Who attended the Philadelphia Convention and how was it organized?

Purpose of Lesson

This lesson will help you understand the reasons for the convention that was held in Philadelphia in the spring of 1787. It will also describe some of the famous Americans who attended the convention and some who did not. Finally, you will learn some of the first decisions made by the Framers.

When you complete this lesson, you should be able to explain why the Philadelphia Convention was held. You should also understand how the Framers organized the convention. Finally, you should be able to describe the contributions of some important Americans who participated in the convention.

Terms to know

Philadelphia Convention
delegate
compromise

Congress starts the process

Imagine that Congress has called for a convention. Each state is invited to send representatives, or **delegates**, to the convention. Congress gives the delegates the responsibility to recommend ways to improve the present government. Who would attend the convention? Where would it be held? What rules would be followed at the convention? Would the public be kept informed of what was happening at the convention?

These were the questions facing the United States in 1787. Congress called for a convention to be held in Philadelphia. Congress told the delegates from the states to develop a plan to improve the Articles of Confederation. The plan was then to be sent to Congress for its approval. As far as Congress was concerned, the men who met in Philadelphia were just advisers to Congress. But something very different was about to happen.

What did Congress tell the delegates in Philadelphia to do? What actually happened?

Write a descriptive slogan for Washington's and Madison's T-shirts.

Fifty-five men: delegates to the Philadelphia Convention

Fifty-five delegates attended the meeting held in Philadelphia. All of them were men. Most were fairly young. Their average age was forty-two. Most had played important roles in the American Revolution. About three-fourths of the Framers had served in Congress. Most were leaders in their states. Some were rich; most were not, but nobody was poor.

Three very important delegates to the convention were George Washington, James Madison, and Benjamin Franklin. Washington was probably the most respected and honored man in the country. He was convinced that a stronger national government was necessary, but he did not talk about it in public. He did not want to become involved in politics. At first, Washington refused to attend the convention. He finally agreed. He was afraid that if he did not, people might think he had lost his faith in republican government.

James Madison is often called the "Father of the Constitution." His influence was great. This was partly because he brought a plan for a stronger national government — called the Virginia Plan — to the convention with him. This plan was used as the basis for discussing how to improve the government. Much of what we know about what happened at the convention is based on Madison's notes.

Benjamin Franklin was 81 and in poor health. He attended the convention as a delegate from Pennsylvania. He was one of the most respected men in America. Franklin had a long and distinguished career as printer, inventor, writer, revolutionary, peacemaker, and diplomat. At the convention, his primary role was encouraging the delegates to cooperate with each other when they disagreed. He also supported the important **compromises** they reached to solve their disagreements. You will learn more about his contributions in later lessons.

Patrick Henry said he did not attend the convention because he "smelled a rat." What do you think he meant by this?

Americans who were not at the convention

Some important Americans did not attend the convention. Thomas Jefferson and Thomas Paine were in France. John Adams was in England. Patrick Henry refused to attend the convention because he was against the creation of a strong national government. He suspected that the delegates might not just try to improve the Articles of Confederation. He was afraid they might try to write a new constitution that created a powerful national government. He was right. After the convention, Patrick Henry worked against ratification of the Constitution.

The delegates to the convention did not represent all parts of the American population. There were no women among the delegates. There were no free black men or slaves present. Poor farmers—like those who took part in Shays' Rebellion—were not present. The Rhode Island state legislature refused to send a delegation to the convention. Citizens there were fiercely independent and hostile to any idea of a new constitution.

The convention begins

By May 25, 1787, delegates from eleven states were present in Philadelphia. George Washington was unanimously elected to preside over the convention. Almost immediately, the Framers agreed on three things:

1. Congress had told them to recommend ways to improve the Articles of Confederation. The Framers decided not to pay any attention to these instructions. They thought the problems with the Articles of Confederation were too serious to try to correct them. So, they began to write a new constitution.

2. They decided to keep the record of what they said at the convention a secret for 30 years. There were two reasons for this:

   • The Framers wanted to develop the best constitution they could. Many were afraid that if their discussions were made public, they would not feel free to express their opinions. They also did not want people outside the convention to try to influence what they were doing.

- The Framers wanted the constitution they developed to be accepted. They thought that it would have a greater chance of being accepted if people did not know about the arguments that went on during its creation.

3. They agreed that each state would have one vote at the convention. This decision was made to gain the cooperation of the small states. Delaware, for example, had threatened to withdraw from the convention if states with large populations were given more votes than states with small populations.

The Framers agreed on a number of basic ideas about government. These included the following ideas:

- They should create a constitutional government, a government of limited powers.

- The purpose of the government should be to protect basic rights and promote the common welfare.

- A strong national government was needed to serve these purposes.

- A republican form of government of elected representatives was necessary to make sure the government served the common welfare.

- The separation of powers and a system of checks and balances were necessary to prevent the abuse of power.

Because of their agreement on basic ideas about government, the Framers were able to write the Constitution. In less than four months they created a constitution that has lasted, with some revisions, for over 200 years.

Reviewing and using the lesson

1. What was the original purpose for calling a meeting in Philadelphia in 1787? Why was the purpose changed? By whose authority was it changed?

2. In what ways were the delegates representative of the American people? In what ways were they not representative?

3. If you were forming a group to write a new constitution today, who would you choose for your group? Explain your answer.

4. Should the topics being debated at the Philadelphia Convention have been reported to the public? Why or why not?

What was the conflict over representation?

Purpose of Lesson

As you learned in the previous lesson, the Framers agreed about the need for a strong national government. They also agreed that the Articles of Confederation needed to be replaced by a new constitution. In this and the following two lessons, you will learn about some of the major ideas the delegates did not agree on.

This lesson deals with the disagreement about how many representatives each state should be able to send to Congress. When you finish this lesson, you should be able to explain this conflict over representation and how it was solved.

Terms to know

equal representation
New Jersey Plan
proportional representation
Virginia Plan
Great Compromise/
Connecticut Compromise
bill
amend

The conflict between the large and small states

One of the most important conflicts among the Framers was about representation in Congress. They disagreed over how many representatives each state should be able to send to Congress. The conflict was between delegates from states with small populations and those from states with large populations. The following were their positions.

- **Small population states.** These states were afraid that the states with larger populations would control the new national government. Their solution was to argue that each state should have the same number of representatives in Congress. This solution was called **equal representation**.

Population of the thirteen original states from the Official Census of 1790	
Connecticut	237,946
Delaware	59,096
Georgia	82,548
Maryland	319,728
Massachusetts	378,787
New Hampshire	141,885
New Jersey	184,139
New York	340,120
North Carolina	393,751
Pennsylvania	434,373
Rhode Island	68,825
South Carolina	249,073
Virginia	691,737

Which states do you think were more likely to have supported equal representation?

The idea of equal representation was contained in a plan created by the delegates from New Jersey. It was called the **New Jersey Plan**. The New Jersey Plan called for only one house of Congress. Each state would have an equal number of representatives in Congress.

- **Large population states.** The delegates from the states with larger populations thought this was unfair. They argued that a state with more people should have more representatives in Congress. Their plan was called **proportional representation** and was a part of Madison's **Virginia Plan**. The Virginia Plan called for two houses in Congress.

The Framers were divided on this issue. They could not reach a decision. Neither side was willing to give in. A special committee of one delegate from each state was asked to develop a solution.

Problem solving

Developing a solution on representation

Your class should be divided into committees of about six students each. Each committee should contain some students who represent the small states and some who represent the large states. The task of each committee is as follows.

1. Meet and develop a plan for the number of representatives each state should be allowed to send to Congress. Should Congress have one or two houses?

2. Select a spokesperson to present your committee's plan to the entire class. All members of the committee may help to clarify the plan and defend it against criticisms by members of the other committees.

3. Each committee may then revise its plan if it wishes, and put it on the board or chart paper.

4. Finally, the entire class should compare the plans made by each committee. The class should try to reach an agreement on the question of representation. Compare the plan you have developed with the plan arrived at by the Framers.

The Great Compromise

The committee appointed by the Framers to solve the problem you have just discussed recommended a compromise known both as the **Great Compromise** and the **Connecticut Compromise**. Its solution, first suggested by Benjamin Franklin, contains three important parts.

- Congress would have two houses, the Senate and the House of Representatives.

- The House of Representatives would be elected on the basis of proportional representation. The House would be given the power to develop all **bills** (proposed laws) for taxing and government spending.

- The Senate would be elected on the basis of equal representation. At first, the Senate was limited to either accepting or rejecting bills for taxing and government spending passed by the House. This was later changed to let the Senate

How did the Great Compromise solve the problem of representation?

amend (change) money bills developed in the House.

As in most compromises, each side received a little and each gave up a little. The small states received equal representation in the Senate. The large states won control of the House of Representatives based on proportional representation. Also, the House was given important powers related to taxing and spending.

The result was that the large states would have slightly more influence over the creation of laws on taxation and how money would be spent. Bills passed by the House could always be checked, or rejected, by the Senate where the small states had equal representation.

The compromise was hotly debated. It finally passed by one vote.

Reviewing and using the lesson

1. Explain the difference between equal representation and proportional representation. Which plan did the states with large populations support? Why?

2. Refer to the chart on page 50. List some of the large and small states that you think were probably on opposite sides of the question on representation.

3. What position would you take on the issue of equal and proprotional representation if it were raised today? Explain your answer.

What were the conflicts between the northern and southern states?

Purpose of Lesson

The states of the North and South had different economies and different economic interests. These differences led to another conflict among the Framers. Two of the major sources of disagreement were over protective tariffs and slavery. When you finish this lesson, you should be able to explain these conflicts and how they were solved.

Terms to know
protective tariff
three-fifths clause
fugitive slave clause

The conflict between the northern and southern states

The economy of the South was almost completely agricultural. People who owned plantations (large farms) in these states depended on slave labor. Slaves were considered property and could be bought or sold. They were not considered citizens and did not have the rights of citizens.

The southern states produced agricultural products such as cotton, tobacco, and indigo. They sold some of these products to the northern states. But many of the products were sold to Great Britain and other nations in Europe. In turn, people in the South bought many of the manufactured goods they needed from Great Britain.

The economy of the North was much more diverse than that of the South. The North's economy generally relied on free labor. This is a system in which a worker and an employer agree on how much the worker will be paid. People earned their living as farmers, fishermen, merchants, or bankers. Others manufactured products or worked as laborers.

The North was also a center of shipbuilding and trade with other nations. For this reason, it was in direct competition with Great Britain's shipping and manufacturing industries.

The conflict over protective tariffs

These economic differences caused a conflict of interest between delegates from the North and South. They disagreed over the issues of **protective tariffs** and **slavery**. Protective tariffs are taxes on products imported from other nations which increase their cost. The different positions of the delegates on protective tariffs were as follows.

- **The northern position.** The northern states believed that protective tariffs were necessary to allow their businesses to be competitive with England's and prosper. Protective tariffs on English products would make them cost more than similar products made in America. As a result, Americans would be more likely to buy goods made in their own country instead of those made in other countries.

Framers from the North wanted the Constitution to give the new national government the power to control trade between the states and trade with foreign nations. This power included giving the national government the power to pass protective tariffs.

- **The southern position.** The South argued that protective tariffs would increase the cost of the manufactured goods which they bought from European nations. They argued that this unfairly favored the North. They were also afraid that England might place tariffs on the South's agricultural products. This would make them harder to sell.

Southern states had fewer citizens than northern states. They were afraid they would be a minority in the Congress of the new government. They might have less power than the northern states in the national government. So they opposed giving the national government power to regulate trade.

The conflict over slavery

The conflict over slavery was more complicated. Slavery had been practiced in many parts of the world for over 2,000 years. It was established in the colonies soon after the first settlements. Many of the Framers were opposed to slavery. Still, some people in the South depended on slaves as workers. Slaves were considered personal property, and slave owners wanted to continue to use them.

Delegates from three southern states said they would refuse to be part of the national government if it denied their citizens the right to own and import slaves. Framers from other states were against slavery, but they wanted to be sure all states would join the Union.

Review the following graph and table which show the free and slave populations of the thirteen states. Discuss the questions following them, and then complete the problem-solving activity.

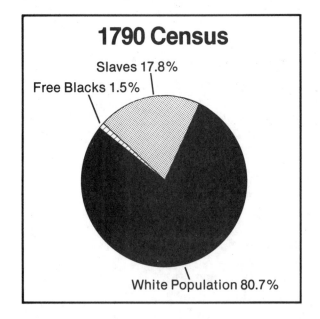

1790 Census

Slaves 17.8%
Free Blacks 1.5%
White Population 80.7%

Slave population of the thirteen original states from the 1790 census		
KEY: Total Population **Slave Population**		
Connecticut	237,946	**2,764**
Delaware	59,096	**8,887**
Georgia	82,548	**29,264**
Maryland	319,728	**103,036**
Massachusetts	378,787	**0**
New Hampshire	141,885	**158**
New Jersey	184,139	**11,423**
New York	340,120	**21,324**
North Carolina	393,751	**100,572**
Pennsylvania	434,373	**3,737**
Rhode Island	68,825	**948**
South Carolina	249,073	**107,094**
Virginia	691,737	**292,627**

Problem solving

Developing compromises to form the Union

Your class should be divided into committees of about five students each. Each committee should contain some students who represent the northern states and some who represent the southern states. The task of each committee is as follows.

1. Meet and develop a plan for dealing with the issues of protective tariffs and slavery. This plan should make it possible for all states to join the Union.

2. Select a spokesperson to present the plan to the entire class. Then, all members of the committee may help to clarify the plan. They should also help defend it against criticisms by members of the other committees.

3. Each committee may then revise its plan, if it wishes, and put it on the chalkboard or chart paper.

The entire class should then compare the plans made by the committees and try to reach an agreement on a plan. After you have completed this exercise, compare the plan you have developed with the plan arrived at by the Framers.

Compromises made to get southern states to sign the Constitution

After considerable debate, the Framers from the North and the South agreed on several compromises. The compromises served the interests of both the northerners who did not own slaves and the southern slaveowners. As in most compromises, each side gave up something in return for getting something it wanted. Read the following parts of Article I of the Constitution. Identify which parts were probably favored by the North and which by the South.

Section Eight. The Congress shall have the power:

1. To lay and collect taxes, duties, imposts, and excises,...

3. To regulate commerce with foreign nations, and among the several states, and with the Indian tribes;

Section Nine. 1. The migration or importation of such persons as any of the states now existing shall think proper to admit, shall not be prohibited by the Congress prior to the year (1808)....

As you can see, the Constitution gave Congress the power to place tariffs on imports. Congress was also given the power to control both interstate and foreign commerce (trade). The power to control trade was very important to the northern states. To get southern approval for this power, the Framers from the North compromised on the question of slavery. They agreed that the national government would not interfere with the slave trade until at least 1808.

The northern delegates also agreed to several more demands of the southern delegates. They agreed that each slave was to be counted as three-fifths of a person. This is the famous **three-fifths clause**. This number was to be used in deciding how many representatives a state could send to the House of Representatives. Each slave was also to be counted as three-fifths of a person for purposes of taxation.

Finally, the northern delegates agreed to add the **fugitive slave clause** in Article IV. It meant that slaves who escaped to other states must be returned to their owners.

These parts of the Constitution were designed to satisfy the demands of the slave-owning states. There were Founders in both the North and the South who were strongly against slavery. For example, one Framer denounced slavery as "... the curse of Heaven on the states..." where it existed. However, the compromises were accepted by a majority of the delegates to get the support of North Carolina, South Carolina, and Georgia. These states would not have supported the Constitution without them. In spite of strong criticisms, these compromises were not as controversial in 1787 as they became in the 1800s.

Reviewing and using the lesson

1. What important differences of opinion existed between the northern and southern states? Which of these do you think was the most controversial? Why?

2. What fundamental ideas about constitutional government were violated by the compromise reached between the northern and southern delegates?

3. Are there other ways that the issue of slavery could have been resolved at the convention? Explain your position.

What was the conflict over the legislative power of the national government?

Purpose of Lesson

One of the major problems facing the Framers was how much power to give to the national government. In this lesson, you will learn about the debates over this problem and how agreement was reached on the powers of Congress—the legislative branch. When you finish this lesson, you should be able to explain how these debates affected the way the Constitution was written. The next lesson will discuss the delegation of power to the executive and judicial branches.

Terms to know
enumerated powers
general welfare clause
necessary and proper clause

How much power should be given to Congress?

The main purpose of the Framers was to create a national government stronger than the one established by the Articles of Confederation. The Framers thought the Articles did not give Congress enough power to deal with trade and economic problems. More importantly, they thought Congress was not strong enough to control the state governments. The Framers were convinced that the state legislatures were passing laws violating the property rights of many citizens.

The basic problem was that under the Articles of Confederation, Congress did not have the power to act directly on the people. If it passed laws, it had to depend on the states to enforce them. Congress could not raise taxes to support itself; it could only ask the states for money. Many states ignored congressional requests for funds.

Most of the Framers agreed on the need for a stronger national government. But there were still some disagreements. The Framers' experience with the government of Great Britain had left many of them very suspicious of national power.

The compromises over representation and slavery greatly reduced resistance to increasing the power of the national government. However, the delegates still disagreed over how much power to give to each of the three branches of the national government. The problem was to create a national government that was

- strong enough to protect the rights of the people (especially property rights), and yet

- not so strong that it would endanger those rights.

How should the Constitution be written to give power to Congress?

The Framers could have written the Constitution in general language. James

Madison argued that the new Congress should have all the powers that it had under the Articles of Confederation. In addition, he wanted Congress to make all laws which the state legislatures were unable to make. He also said Congress should be given the power to veto laws made by state legislatures. These recommendations would have given the national government a large amount of power over the states and the people. Some delegates agreed with Madison.

Many of the Framers disagreed with him. They saw a problem with general language in the Constitution. General language could be interpreted to give the government the power to do almost anything it wanted to do. It does not provide a good way to limit the powers of government. They also opposed giving Congress the power to veto laws made by state legislatures. Under British rule, royal governors and Parliament had vetoed acts of the colonial legislatures. The Framers did not want to give this power to Congress.

One alternative was to use very specific language in the Constitution. This would be to write down exactly what the Congress could and could not do. The problem with such specific language was that it might leave out important powers needed by Congress to deal with unforeseen situations.

The Framers' solution was to use both general and specific language. The Constitution would give specific powers to Congress and place limitations on these powers. It would also include two general clauses which would give Congress the power to deal with unexpected situations.

Specific powers of Congress

Article I deals with the powers of Congress. It takes up more than half the Constitution—which shows how important it was to the Framers. Article I, section 8 includes seventeen specific, or **enumerated powers**. Some of these powers are the right of Congress:

- to impose and collect taxes and duties
- to borrow money
- to regulate commerce with foreign nations and among the states
- to coin money (create a national currency)
- to establish post offices
- to declare war and to raise an army and navy

General powers of Congress

Article I, section 8 also includes two important general statements of power given to Congress. These give Congress the power to

- "... provide for the common defense and **general welfare** of the United States....", and

- make all laws which shall be "**necessary and proper**" for carrying out the other powers that have been given to Congress. For example, the Constitution gives Congress the power to maintain an army and navy. The necessary and proper clause gives it the power to pass those laws that are necessary to do this. These might include the power to pass laws requiring citizens to serve in the armed forces.

What are the responsibilities of the legislative branch of government?

A source of conflict

The general welfare and necessary and proper clauses have allowed the Congress to greatly increase its powers. As a result, today the national government has far more power than most of the Framers could have imagined.

These clauses did not cause any disagreements at the convention. However, they caused strong disagreements during the debates over the ratification of the Constitution. They also resulted in conflicts in the early years of the new government. You will learn more about these conflicts in later lessons.

Problem solving

Creating bills that are constitutional

A bill is a proposed law. Members of Congress create bills and try to get a majority of both houses to vote for them. If this happens, the bill is sent to the President for his approval. If the President approves a bill, it becomes a law. If the President vetoes a bill, it can only become a law if two-thirds of both houses of Congress vote for it after the veto.

Your class should be divided into congressional committees of about five members each. Complete the following activity and report your findings to the entire class.

Your committee wants to introduce several bills in Congress. The following are the purposes of some bills you are considering. Review the general and specific powers granted to Congress. For each bill, make an argument that Article I, section 8 does or does not give Congress the power to pass it. Then develop answers for the questions that follow.

- A bill that allows the United States Treasury to borrow money by selling savings bonds.

- A bill that allows the executive branch to draft citizens to serve in the armed forces.

- A bill that allows the executive branch to conduct a space exploration program.

- A bill that allows the executive branch to fine industries that pollute the air.

- A bill that requires the executive branch to use tax money to provide medical assistance to older citizens who cannot pay for it themselves.

1. Consider the powers given Congress by Article I, section 8. Create three bills that you think Congress could not pass under that Article. Explain why you think so.

2. Explain what problems might arise because of the way Article I, section 8 is written.

What does Article I do?

Article I strengthened the powers of Congress. If you review Article I you will see it lists the powers of Congress and limits on those powers. In this way, the Framers tried to balance the need for a strong government with the need to limit its powers. Those limits were included to make sure that the government did not become a threat to the people's rights.

Article I, section 9 limits the power of Congress. It lists things Congress cannot do. For example, Congress is not allowed to create a class of nobles. Members of the government cannot accept titles of nobility from foreign governments. This shows how important the Framers thought it was for republican government to treat all citizens equally.

Article I, section 10 limits the powers of state governments. It lists things state governments cannot do. For example, states cannot tax the import or export of goods. They cannot declare and carry out a war. This section increased the power of the national government in relation to the state governments.

Reviewing and using the lesson

1. What experiences of the Framers might have influenced their ideas about how much power they should give the national government? Give examples of some of these experiences.

2. Why do you think the Framers devoted so much of the Constitution to the legislative branch?

3. Read Article I, section 9 of the Constitution. What do you think was the purpose of each of the limitations listed?

How much power should be given to the executive and judicial branches?

Purpose of Lesson

The Framers believed that separation of powers and checks and balances were essential to protect the rights of the people. They had to decide which powers to give to each of the branches of the national government. And they had to decide how to give each branch ways to check the powers of the other branches.

In this lesson you will learn about the problems the Framers had in deciding how much power to give to the executive and judicial branches. You will also learn how they provided ways these branches could check the power of the legislative branch. Finally, you will learn about the special system the Framers established for the election of the President.

Terms to know

impeach
electoral college
original jurisdiction
appellate jurisdiction
supremacy clause

How much power should be given to the executive branch?

As you have learned, in most of the state governments the legislative branch was given more power than the executive branch. Many of the Framers, such as Madison and Washington, thought that legislative supremacy was dangerous. They believed that majorities in a number of state legislatures had passed laws which violated the natural rights of minorities.

At the same time, the Framers still remembered how much trouble they had had with the executive branch of the British government. They believed the king and royal governors had violated their rights. The problem at the Philadelphia Convention was to create an executive branch that

- had enough power to fulfill its responsibilities, and yet

- was not so strong that it could overwhelm the other branches and endanger the rights of the people.

The Framers' solution

The Framers' solution is in Article II of the Constitution, which creates the executive branch. Article II is written in general terms so it gives broad powers to the President. The executive branch was given powers the Framers thought could be most efficiently exercised by a single person— the President. These include the power to enforce laws made by Congress, make treaties with foreign nations, appoint certain important officials, and conduct wars. One of the most important powers the President has under the Constitution is the power to veto laws passed by Congress.

The Framers wanted to balance the powers of the President and Congress. They limited the powers of the executive branch by making it share most of its powers with Congress. Here are some examples of how this works.

- **Appointments**. The President has the power to nominate people for important jobs in the executive branch. He also nominates people to serve in the judicial branch of the national government. However, the Senate has the power to accept or reject these nominations.

- **Treaties.** The President has the power to enter into a treaty with another nation. The treaty must be approved or rejected by the Senate.

- **War**. Although the President can conduct a war as Commander-in-Chief, only Congress can declare war. In addition, Congress has the power to provide money for the war.

- **Veto.** The President may veto laws passed by Congress. Congress, however, may override the veto by a two-thirds vote of both houses.

The Constitution provides another important way to control the President and prevent the abuse of power. It gives the House of Representatives the power to **impeach** the President. This means the House can accuse the President of serious crimes. The Senate can then put the President on trial. If he is found guilty, he is removed from office.

Only one President, Andrew Johnson, has ever been charged and put on trial. He was found innocent. Another President, Richard Nixon, was threatened with impeachment proceedings. He eventually resigned. While it has rarely been used, impeachment is an important congressional power for controlling the executive branch.

How does this picture illustrate the responsibilities of the executive branch of government?

How should the President be selected?

Article II of the Constitution is short compared to Article I. The list of powers given to the President is brief, but these powers are very important.

The Framers had given great powers to the President. It is not surprising that they were concerned about how people were to be selected to fill this position. They took it for granted that George Washington would be the first President, and he was their model. They thought he was patriotic, honest, devoted to the public good, and not interested in using power for his own advantage.

The Framers tried to develop a way of selecting future Presidents who would be as qualified as Washington. They discussed this problem for some time. They also discussed how long a President should be able to stay in office.

It was finally agreed that the President would serve for four years and could be re-elected any number of times. (This was changed in 1951 when the Constitution was amended. The President can now be re-elected only once.)

There were only a few delegates who seriously suggested that the President be chosen directly by the people. Most agreed with Madison's opinion. He thought that the people did not have enough wisdom to be given the right to select a President. He also believed they would not be able to know enough about the candidates to make good choices.

In most states the head of the executive branch was chosen by the state legislature. But the Framers thought that if the President were chosen by the Congress, Congress would be able to control the President. This would result in a weak executive branch. They also thought that if the President were to be selected by the state governments, they would be able to control the President. This would also result in a weak executive branch. Either of these choices would not have helped them create a stronger national government.

The method the Framers finally created for electing the President is a complicated one. An **electoral college** would be created once every four years to choose the President. Each state would have electors equal to the number of Senators and Representatives it had in Congress. Each state was left the power to decide how it would select persons to serve as "electors" in the college.

The person who received a majority of votes in the electoral college would become President.

While we still have the electoral college today, it works quite differently from the way it was orginally established. If they were living today, most of the Framers would be surprised at how we select a President. Political campaigns, with candidates asking the people to vote for them, were not a part of political life in the 18th century.

How much power should be given to the judicial branch?

To complete the system of separation of powers, the Framers planned for a judicial branch. They had fewer problems agreeing on this branch. Most of them agreed on certain ideas about a national court system.

- Judges should be independent of politics so they can use their best judgment to decide cases and not be influenced by political pressures. The best way to do this was to have judges appointed, not elected. Judges could keep their positions "during good behavior." They could not be removed unless they were impeached. They would have to be tried and convicted of "treason, bribery, or other high crimes and misdemeanors." This meant most judges could keep their jobs for life.

- A national judiciary was needed to decide disputes between state governments and between citizens of two or more states. It was also needed to decide disputes between the national government and a state or a citizen.

- There should be a single Supreme Court with two types of jurisdiction, or authority, to hear cases:

1. The Supreme Court would have **original jurisdiction** in cases involving a state government or an ambassador. Original jurisdiction means that these types of cases would go directly to the Supreme Court and not be tried first in a lower court.

2. In all other cases the Supreme Court would have **appellate jurisdiction**. Appellate jurisdiction means that the Supreme Court can choose to hear any case that has already been heard in a lower court.

The Framers clearly intended to give the Supreme Court the power to overrule state laws which violated the Constitution or federal laws. The power is based on the

What does this picture tell you about what the judicial branch does?

supremacy clause in Article VI which states:

> This Constitution, and the laws of the United States...shall be the supreme law of the land; and the judges in every State shall be bound thereby....

The new national government

The Constitution gave the national government the power to act directly upon the people. This was different from the government under the Articles of Confederation. It could only act upon the state governments.

The Constitution also says that the national government is supreme in those areas where it has been given the right to act. For example, suppose a state passes a law allowing its factories to pollute the air. Then Congress passes a law controlling the amount of pollution a factory can produce. Since the national government is supreme, its laws would have to be obeyed over the state laws.

Washington, Madison, and the others who agreed with them got the strong national government they wanted. But the battle was not yet won. There were many people in the United States who were still afraid of a strong national government. They believed that it would be a threat to their rights and to their state governments.

Reviewing and using the lesson

1. How was the Framers' view of the executive branch affected by their knowledge of history and their own experience?

2. According to the Constitution, what is the supreme law of the land? Whose responsibility is it to enforce, or carry out, the laws of the United States?

3. Why did the Framers make the executive branch share some of its powers with Congress?

4. Why do you think the Framers wanted to protect the judicial branch from political influence? What might be the advantages and disadvantages of doing this?

What opinions did the Framers have of the Constitution?

Purpose of Lesson

This lesson focuses on the opinions of two of the Framers about the new Constitution. Benjamin Franklin argued in favor of the Constitution and urged all the delegates to sign it. George Mason, a Virginia delegate, argued against the new plan of government. In fact, he was one of the three delegates who stayed until the end of the convention but refused to sign the document.

When you have completed this lesson you should be able to explain Franklin's reasons for supporting the Constitution. You should also be able to explain George Mason's arguments against the Constitution.

Terms to know

pardon
treason
simple majority vote
bill of rights

Franklin urges acceptance of the Constitution

When the Framers left the convention, they did not believe they had created a perfect plan of government. The four months they had spent putting it together had been filled with disagreements. Some delegates, such as Alexander Hamilton, had walked out of the convention. (He did return to sign the Constitution.) A few others refused to sign the Constitution. The great majority, however, thought they had done the best they could.

On September 17, 1787, the last day of the convention, Benjamin Franklin made his feelings known to all the delegates. He was too weak to deliver his speech. He asked James Wilson, a fellow delegate from Pennsylvania, to read it for him. Franklin encouraged all the delegates to sign the Constitution. The following is a summary of what he said.

- He did not agree with everything that had been included in the Constitution. But, at the same time, he doubted his ability to know more than the rest of the delegates.

- He was willing to accept the Constitution because he believed a national government was necessary.

- He did not believe that any other group of men could create a better plan of government than the delegates who had worked so hard throughout that summer in Philadelphia.

- He praised the delegates for their cooperation. He also praised them for overcoming their own prejudices, strong feelings about some issues, errors of opinion, special interests, and selfish views.

How does this picture illustrate Franklin's opinion of the Constitution?

- He congratulated the other delegates for having produced what he believed might be the best plan of government ever designed.

- He warned of the harmful effects that might result both in the United States and among foreign nations, if the delegates let people know of their objections to the Constitution.

- He asked the other delegates to consider, as he had, the possibility that their objections might not be as good as they thought they were.

- Finally, Franklin encouraged all of the delegates to sign the Constitution to show their support.

George Mason's objections to the Constitution

George Mason was a leading delegate from Virginia. He was the author of the Virginia Bill of Rights. Mason and Patrick Henry were famous for their support of the rights of the people and of the states. James Madison said that Mason had "the greatest talent for debate of any man he had ever seen or heard speak."

Mason attended the convention to the end. He did not support the finished Constitution. Before the convention ended, Mason wrote his objections on the blank pages of his copy of the Constitution. His list filled three pages. Some of his most important criticisms are summarized below:

- Senators were to be selected by state legislatures and not elected by the people. This meant that Senators would not represent the people or be responsible to them.

- The President was given the power to make treaties with the approval of the Senate. These treaties would become the supreme law of the land. This allowed the President and the Senate to create laws without the approval of the House of Representatives. The people would not have an adequate voice in the making of treaties.

- Too much power was given to the President and the Senate. The Senate had the power to try the President and other members of government in cases of impeachment. These two branches of government were not directly elected by the people. The House of Representatives, which was elected by the people, would be helpless in the face of the greater power of the President and Senate.

- The national judicial branch was given so much power it could destroy the state courts by overruling them. If this were to happen, the poor would not be able to afford to use the federal courts. The rich would then have an advantage they could use to oppress and ruin the poor.

- The President was given the power to grant **pardons** (forgiveness) for acts of **treason** (aiding the enemy). This made it possible for a President to protect individuals who may have been acting for him. In this way, the President could prevent the discovery of his own guilt.

- The requirement of a **simple majority vote** (one more than half)

George Mason was one of the three delegates who refused to sign the Constitution.
Which of his objections would you rank as most important? Why?

68

by each house of Congress on commercial and trade laws completely favored the eight northern states. The agricultural interests of the five southern states could not be protected. This might eventually mean economic ruin for the South.

- The necessary and proper clause gave Congress unlimited power to make any laws it chose. Congress could eventually increase its power as much as it wanted to. The power of the state legislatures could eventually be eliminated by the acts of Congress. Congress could create commercial monopolies, new types of crimes, or inflict unusual and severe punishment on the citizenry.

George Mason had also made other criticisms of the Constitution during the convention. Some of them were accepted at the time, and others resulted in changes made after the convention ended. One of the most notable of his criticisms was that the Constitution did not contain a **bill of rights**. This is a list of rights that the government cannot take from the people. The story of how and why the Bill of Rights was added to the Constitution is told in a following lesson.

Problem solving

Your class should be divided into seven groups. Each group should be assigned to study one of George Mason's objections. Groups should then:

- Take and defend a position for or against the objection. It may be supported by identifying events in American history that illustrate the objection the group is studying.

- Identify any constitutional checks and balances or other provisions that could be used to respond to his criticisms.

Groups should then share their findings with the class.

Reviewing and using the lesson

1. Describe Benjamin Franklin's attitude toward the Constitution. In your opinion, which of his reasons for signing the Constitution do you think might have been most persuasive to the other delegates?

2. Rank in order from most important to least important the arguments of George Mason. Explain your reasons for selecting your choices.

Who were the supporters and critics of the Constitution?

Purpose of Lesson

In this lesson you will learn about the struggle to get the Constitution ratified by the states. You will examine the plan developed by the supporters of the Constitution, called the Federalists, to get it ratified. You will also look at the major arguments used by the Anti-Federalists, the opponents of the Constitution, to keep the new plan of government from being approved.

When you have completed this lesson you should be able to describe the differences between the arguments of the Federalists and the Anti-Federalists. You should also be able to explain the ratification process that followed the convention.

Terms to know

ratified
ratifying conventions
The Federalist
Anti-Federalists
Federalists

What happened after the Philadelphia Convention?

Imagine that you were a member of the group that had just written the Constitution. You know that many leaders in Congress and the state governments will be against it.

However, the Constitution was written in secret, so the opponents do not know everything that is included in the final version. They have not yet had time to prepare all their arguments against the Constitution.

What plan would you develop for getting the Constitution **ratified**, or formally approved? Who do you think should have the right to vote for ratification? How soon should the ratification process take place? These are some of the questions raised by the Framers as the convention drew to a close.

The Framers ask the voters to approve the Constitution

James Madison developed the plan for ratifying the Constitution. He was afraid that the Constitution would be rejected if either the Congress or the state legislatures were asked to ratify it. To avoid this, he thought that the best plan was to get the voters of each state to ratify the Constitution. The Constitution would be presented at special **ratifying conventions** to be held in each state. The delegates to these conventions would be elected by popular vote of the people for the sole purpose of approving the Constitution.

Madison's plan was based on the idea contained in the Preamble to the Constitution, which says, "We the People...do ordain and establish this Constitution...." The people who were to be governed by the new national government were asked to consent to its creation and to agree to obey its decisions. Thus, the Constitution can be considered a social contract—an agreement among the people to create a government.

The Framers approved this plan. They included Article VII which said the Constitution would be in effect after it had been ratified by the conventions of nine of the thirteen states. They only required approval of the voters of nine states because they were afraid they could not get approval of all thirteen.

Once they had agreed upon their plan, the people who supported the Constitution went to work. They encouraged the states to organize and elect delegates to the state ratifying conventions as quickly as possible. They knew that the opponents of the Constitution had not had much time to prepare their arguments. By contrast, the supporters of the Constitution had worked on it for almost four months. They knew the arguments for and against it. They thought if the state conventions acted quickly, the Constitution would be ratified before its opponents could organize.

The struggle for ratification

The **Federalists** were people who supported the Constitution and wanted it ratified. The **Anti-Federalists** were people who fought against the Constitution. The Anti-Federalists put up a strong fight even though the Federalists had a head start on them. The debates in the states over ratification lasted ten months. It was an intense, and sometimes bitter, political struggle.

One of the most difficult fights was in New York. To help the Federalist cause, Alexander Hamilton, James Madison, and John Jay wrote a series of articles supporting ratification. These articles, now called *The Federalist,* appeared in a New York newspaper. They were also used in the Virginia ratification debates.

Anti-Federalist leaders included George Mason, Edmund Randolph, and Elbridge Gerry. Each had attended the Philadelphia Convention but refused to sign the document. John Hancock, Samuel Adams, and Richard Henry Lee were all leading revolutionaries and signers of the Declaration of Independence. They also fought against ratification of the Constitution. Patrick Henry had always opposed the idea of a strong national government. He became a leading Anti-Federalist at the Virginia ratifying convention. Mercy Otis Warren, a playwright, also opposed ratification. She, like the others, wrote pamphlets explaining why she did not support the Constitution.

The following section describes some of the arguments used by the two sides in the ratification struggle.

Arguments for and against the Constitution

Many arguments were made both for and against the Constitution. Most of them had to do with three basic questions: (1) whether the new Constitution would maintain a republican form of government, (2) whether the national government would have too much power, and (3) whether a bill of rights was needed in the Constitution.

The following chart will help you identify the arguments of the Federalists and Anti-Federalists.

Positions on the Constitution

Anti-Federalists	Federalists
Throughout history, the only places where republican governments had worked had been small communities. In those communities, the people had been about equal in wealth and had held the same values. People who are not too rich or too poor are more likely to possess civic virtue and to agree on what is best for their common welfare. The new nation was so large and diverse that people would not be able to agree on their common welfare.	History has proven that all of the small republics of the past had been destroyed by selfish groups. The civic virtue of the citizens had not been enough to prevent them from seeking their own selfish interests rather than working for the common welfare. A large republic, where the government was organized on the basis of checks and balances, and power was divided between the national and the state governments, would be better. Under such a government, it would be more difficult for special interests to attain their goals and violate the common welfare.
Free government requires the active participation of the people. The national government would be located too far from most people's communities to allow them to participate. As a result, the only way the government would be able to rule would be through the use of military force. The result would be a tyranny.	The national government would be so good at protecting the rights of the people that it would soon gain their loyalty and support. It could not become a tyranny because of the limitations placed on it by the system of checks and balances and separation of powers.
The Constitution gives the national government too much power at the expense of the state governments. It gives the government the power to tax citizens and to raise and keep an army. The supremacy clause means all the national government's laws are superior to laws made by the states. As a result, it would only be a matter of time until the state governments were destroyed.	It is true that the national government would have greater power than it did under the Articles of Confederation. But its powers are limited to tasks that face the entire nation, such as trade, currency, and defense. Experience has shown that a stronger national government is needed to deal with these problems. The Constitution provides adequate protections for the state governments to prevent their being destroyed by the national government.
The necessary and proper clause is too general and, as a result, gives too much power to the national government. It is dangerous not to list the powers of the government in order to put clear limits on them.	The necessary and proper and general welfare clauses are necessary if the national government is to do the things it is responsible for doing.

The Constitution gives too much power to the executive branch of government. It would soon become a monarchy.	A strong executive branch is necessary for the national government to be able to fulfill its responsibilities. The powers of the national government are separated and balanced among the three branches so no one can dominate the others. The Constitution gives the Congress and the Supreme Court ways to check the use of power by the executive branch so it cannot become a monarchy.
The Constitution does not include a bill of rights which is essential for protecting individuals against the power of the national government.	A bill of rights is unnecessary because the powers of the government are limited. A bill of rights would give the impression that the people could only expect protection of those rights that were actually listed.

What slogans might the Federalists and Anti-Federalists be using? Write one of your own.

The agreement to add a bill of rights

A compromise was reached on the issue of a bill of rights. The Federalists made this compromise to get enough support for the Constitution so it would be ratified. They agreed that when the first Congress was held, it would draft a bill of rights.

The argument to add a bill of rights was a victory for the Anti-Federalists. It was an important addition to the Constitution and has been of great importance in the protection of the basic rights of the American people.

Reviewing and using the lesson

1. Who were the Federalists? Who were the Anti-Federalists?

2. Why didn't the Federalists want the Constitution submitted to the existing Congress or state governments for ratification?

3. How did the Federalists answer the criticism that the Constitution gave the federal government too much power?

4. The Anti-Federalists lost their battle to prevent the adoption of the Constitution. However, their struggle left a permanent impact on the Constitution. How was this accomplished?

5. Explain what you think were the best reasons for ratification. Then, explain what you think were the best reasons against ratification.

6. Would you have voted to ratify the Constitution as written in 1787? Explain your answer.

Unit Four: How was the Constitution used to establish our government?

How does this picture illustrate the purpose of Unit Four?

Purpose of Unit Four

It is important to understand that the Framers wrote the Constitution as a general framework or plan for the new government. They left out many of the details they knew would have to be added by future presidents and members of Congress. This unit will help you understand how the first government was organized under the Constitution. It will also tell you about some of the unexpected developments that have influenced the way our nation is governed today.

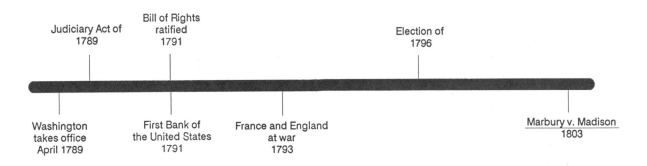

Judiciary Act of 1789

Bill of Rights ratified 1791

Election of 1796

Washington takes office April 1789

First Bank of the United States 1791

France and England at war 1793

Marbury v. Madison 1803

What was the federal system created by the Constitution?

Purpose of Lesson

In this lesson you will learn how the Constitution established a new way to organize a government, a federal system. When you finish this lesson, you should be able to explain what a federal system is and how it differs from other forms of government. You should also be able to identify some of the strengths and weaknesses of a federal system. Finally, you should be able to explain why you think the Framers created such a system of government.

Terms to know

unitary government
confederation
authority
sovereignty
federalism
federal system

Different kinds of government

Before our government was established under the Constitution, most nations had been organized in one of two ways.

- **Unitary governments** were those in which central governments acted directly upon their citizens. Local and state governments received their powers from the central government and were under its control. As a result, central governments were much stronger than local and state governments. Great Britain had a unitary form of government.

- **Confederations** were central governments organized for such limited purposes as defense and regulation of trade. The state governments in a confederation kept full control over anything that affected their own citizens and territory. The separate states were considered stronger than the central government. The United States under the Articles of Confederation had a confederate form of government.

In contrast to these ways of organizing a government, the Constitution created a **federal system** of government. To understand the difference between a federal system and unitary and confederate systems, complete the following problem-solving activity.

What is a federal system?

Your class should be divided into small groups. The illustration below shows how a federal system of government works. Each group should examine the illustration and answer the questions that follow. Each group should then share its answers with the rest of the class.

- Where does power come from in this system of government?

- Who is power given to?

- What are the main differences between federal, unitary, and confederate systems of government?

- Why do you think the Framers chose this system of government?

A new kind of government

The government created by the Framers differed in the following two important ways from other existing systems of government. To understand these differences we must introduce a new term—**authority**. We will define authority as the right to govern. According to the natural rights philosophy, people have the right, or authority, to govern themselves. They also have the right, or authority, to create a government and give it the right to govern them. These ideas were used by the Framers in creating a federal system.

1. **Sovereignty,** or the ultimate authority of the government, is held by the people. The Constitution begins with the words "We the People of the United States..." The people have created the government and given it the authority to govern them. However, the people have the

What does this picture tell you about how the federal system works?

final or ultimate authority to control their government by the means provided in the Constitution.

In most other nations of that time, the government held the ultimate authority. This was true even if the government had originally received its authority from the people. For example, in some countries the king was sovereign. In Great Britain, the Parliament was sovereign. In the United States, the people are sovereign.

2. **Federalism.** The second major difference is that the Constitution provides for a **federal system** of government. In a federal system the people do not delegate, or give, all power to one central government. Instead, they delegate some power to their national government, some to their state governments, and they keep some powers, or rights, for themselves.

The distribution of power in the federal system

The following are examples of how power is distributed in our federal system.

- **Powers to the national or federal government.** As citizens of the nation, the people give certain powers to the federal government. These powers are described in the Constitution. They include the power to create post offices, control interstate and foreign trade, declare and conduct war, and create a national currency.

- **Powers to state governments.** As citizens in the various states, the people give certain powers to their state governments. These powers are listed in each state's constitution. They include the power to control trade within the state, establish public schools, create motor vehicle laws, and control marriage and divorce practices.

- **Powers kept by the people.** Finally, certain rights and powers have been kept by the people and not delegated to any government. They include the right to believe what we wish, select our careers, choose our friends, travel, and raise a family.

It is important to know that in our federal system the federal and state government share certain powers. For example, both governments have the power to tax citizens and businesses and to provide for the health and welfare of the people.

The supremacy of the federal government

There were many disagreements among the Framers over what powers the federal government should have. However, they did agree that the powers of the federal government were to be greater than those of the state governments. This is clearly stated in the supremacy clause of Article VI. The states cannot make laws that conflict with the Constitution or laws made by Congress.

Conflicts between federal and state governments

In our federal system, Congress can make laws governing the people. The state governments can also make laws governing the people. You can imagine that in this kind of system, there will be many times when state laws conflict with those made by Congress. In one instance, these conflicts led to a war between the states — the Civil War.

The Framers created a new and very complicated form of government. They could not predict exactly what powers the state and federal governments would eventually have. Early in our history, the state governments were very powerful. Today, the federal government has far more power over the state governments than most of the Framers could have imagined.

In thinking about the relationship between the federal and state governments, it is important to understand the following things.

- In spite of the increase in the power of the federal government, most of the laws that affect us directly are state laws. These include laws regarding education, most property law, contract law, family law, and criminal law.

- In most cases it is Congress that decides how much power will be left to the states. Congress makes its decisions on the basis of practical and political issues. Voters can influence these decisions.

In developing a federal system of government, the Framers invented a new way to organize a government. In this system, sovereignty remains with the people. The people give certain limited powers to the federal and state governments. Each level of government has the authority to act directly upon the people.

This complicated system is sometimes not as efficient as a unitary system of government. The Framers did not see this as a disadvantage. In fact, they considered it was one of the advantages of federalism. The Framers thought that the separation of powers between the federal and state governments was one way to protect the rights of the people.

Reviewing and using the lesson

1. Explain what a federal system is. Draw a diagram that shows how the federal system works in the United States.

2. Suppose you were in a situation, like that of the Framers, where you were organizing a government. Explain what you think might be some of the advantages and disadvantages of a federal system of government. Which responsibilities and powers would you give to the federal government? Which powers would you give to the state governments? Which powers would you keep for yourselves?

3. Why do you suppose the Framers created a federal system instead of continuing their confederation or creating a unitary system?

4. Define "sovereignty." Who has sovereignty in the United States? Give evidence to support your answer.

5. Discuss what problems might arise from different states passing different laws regarding:
   - crime
   - education
   - employment
   - housing
   - welfare benefits

79

How was the new government established?

Purpose of Lesson

The Constitution was only a plan for the new government. Once it was ratified, it was the job of the first Congress to use this plan to organize the government. By May, 1789, members of the new Congress of the national government were at work in New York City, the nation's temporary capital. In this lesson you will read about some of the decisions made by the first Congress. You will learn how Congress organized the executive branch. You will also learn how Congress established a system of federal courts below the Supreme Court. Finally, you will learn how the Bill of Rights was added to the Constitution.

Terms to know

cabinet
Judiciary Act of 1789
appellate court

The first President

Everyone took it for granted that George Washington would be the first President. He was the most widely respected man in America. However, Washington did not really want to be President. He would have preferred to remain at Mount Vernon and take care of his plantation. But Washington had a strong sense of civic responsibility and felt it was his duty to serve his country. He wrote that "when I had judged...that it was my duty to embark again on the tempestuous and uncertain Ocean of public life, I gave up all expectations of private happiness in this world."

When the votes of the state electors were counted, Washington, as expected, was elected President. John Adams of Massachusetts was chosen as Vice President. Washington took the oath of office on April 30, 1789.

Washington knew that the Founders who were against the Constitution were afraid that it gave too much power to the President. He knew he should not do anything that added to their fears. Yet he also knew that he had to be a strong leader.

Why was Washington elected as the first President?

Many people in Congress were worried about how Washington would use his power. They even disagreed on what they should call the President. Some people said he should be called "His Highness, the President of the United States of America." But, Congress decided, America was not a monarchy and Washington should simply be addressed as "The President of the United States."

Organizing the executive branch

Washington could not run the executive branch alone. The Constitution gives Congress the power to organize the executive branch. To do this, Congress created three departments to help Washington fulfill his responsibilities. These departments and the people Washington chose to lead them are as follows:

- **Department of State.** Thomas Jefferson was selected to serve as Secretary of State to be responsible for the foreign relations of the nation.

- **Department of the Treasury.** Alexander Hamilton, as Secretary of the Treasury, guided the new government in money matters.

- **Department of War.** Henry Knox, as the Secretary of War, handled military affairs and defense.

In addition, Congress created the office of attorney general whose job was to give the President legal advice. Washington appointed Edmund Randolph to this position.

These officials were used by Washington as advisers to help him make decisions. They became known as his **cabinet.** The cabinet positions have grown from these original four to the present number of thirteen. In fact, the executive branch of the federal government has grown far beyond the expectations of the Framers. There are now more people working in the executive branch than were living in the United States at the time of the American Revolution.

Who were the members of Washington's cabinet?

How does this picture illustrate our court system as a result of the Judiciary Act of 1789?

Organizing the judicial branch

Congress not only helped to organize the executive branch of government, it also helped set up the judicial branch. Article III of the Constitution provided for a Supreme Court and said that Congress could establish lower courts as needed.

Congress passed the **Judiciary Act of 1789** which organized the court system for the new nation. A chief justice was to lead the Supreme Court, which would also have five associate justices. Over time, Congress has increased the size of the Court to nine justices.

The Judiciary Act also created a system of lower courts. It included federal district courts to hear cases involving the Constitution or federal laws. Under certain circumstances, if a case was lost in district court, it could be appealed to a higher court. These were known as **appellate courts**. The Judiciary Act established the Supreme Court as the highest court of appeals in the nation. In addition to the federal courts, each state had its own courts established by its legislature to rule on state laws.

The Bill of Rights

When the Constitution was sent to the states for ratification, some people opposed it because it did not include a bill of rights. The Federalists claimed that a bill of rights was not necessary. They said that the Constitution organized the government in such a way that it would be impossible to violate people's rights. They also argued that listing individual rights might make people think that these were the only ones guaranteed by the government.

Finally, a compromise was reached. The Federalists agreed that when the first Congress met, it would draft a bill of rights to be added to the Constitution.

The Bill of Rights was passed by the first Congress. It contains ten amendments. The first eight list basic protections that had already been guaranteed in most of the state constitutions. Some of the most important of these include:

- freedom of religion
- freedom of the press
- freedom of speech
- the rights of assembly and petition
- the right to a speedy, public trial by jury

The Ninth Amendment states that the listing of certain rights does not mean that these are the only rights the people have. Finally, the Tenth Amendment states that the powers not given to the federal government by the Constitution, nor forbidden by the Constitution to the states, belong to the states or to the people.

The Bill of Rights was proposed by Congress in 1789 and ratified by the necessary eleven states on December 15, 1791. It has proved to be very important to the protection of the basic rights of the American people. You will learn more about the Bill of Rights in the next unit.

Reviewing and using the lesson

1. The Constitution describes the organization of the executive and judicial branches only in general terms. How did the first Congress organize these two branches of the government?

2. The idea of having one person serve as President was developed when our nation had less than four million people. Today we have more than 240 million people. Do you think it is still a good idea to have only one person head the executive branch? Why or why not? What alternatives can you suggest?

3. What was the purpose of the Bill of Rights? Why was it included in our Constitution?

How did political parties develop?

Purpose of Lesson

When George Washington was elected as the first President, he received every electoral vote. One reason for this was the great respect people had for him. Another reason was that there were no political parties to run candidates against him.

In this lesson you will learn of some of the problems faced by the new nation. You will also learn how different groups of people thought these problems should be resolved.

When you have finished this lesson you should be able to describe what political parties are, how they first began in American politics, and what purpose they serve today. You should also be able to describe the two original political parties and their leaders.

Terms to know

faction
political parties
Federalist Party
Republican Party

Why the Framers were against political parties

In one of his most famous essays in *The Federalist,* James Madison argued that the Constitution would control **factions.** He defined a faction as a group of citizens that pursues its own selfish interests without thinking of the common welfare. The Framers believed that factions were dangerous for republican government, whose purpose is to promote the common welfare.

The Framers thought that **political parties,** groups of people who join together because they have similar views about government, were factions. If parties became part of the political system, they would fight to promote the interests of their own members. The Framers feared that the strongest political party would then control the government. Under such circumstances, the government would not equally protect the rights and interests of all the people. It would instead promote the interests of the party in power.

The new nation faced many problems during its early years. The country was in debt. It needed to establish relations with other nations. The government needed treaties with the Native Americans in the West. There were different opinions about solving these problems. As Washington and his advisers tried to deal with the issues, disagreements arose. These disagreements eventually led to the development of political parties.

Disagreements between the Federalists and Republicans

Two of George Washington's advisers, Thomas Jefferson and Alexander Hamilton, had very different ideas about government.

Hamilton wanted a strong national government. He believed the Constitution protected the rights of the people because it limited the powers of the federal government. However, within these limitations, he favored a **broad** view of the meaning of the Constitution. Hamilton's interpretation would give more power to the federal government than many other people believed it should have. Hamilton and his supporters became known as the **Federalist Party**.

Suppose Hamilton had drawn this picture. What view would Hamilton be expressing?

Hamilton was opposed by Thomas Jefferson who believed in small, local government. He and his followers were afraid that the federal government would become too powerful and threaten the rights of the people. They were worried that a broad interpretation of the Constitution would give too much power to the national government. Because of this fear, they favored a **narrow** view of the meaning of the Constitution. This meant interpreting the Constitution to limit the powers of the federal government.

Suppose Jefferson had drawn this picture. What view would Jefferson be expressing?

Jefferson and his supporters were called **Republicans** (this party became the Democratic party of today). They were especially worried about two parts of the Constitution. They were afraid that the necessary and proper and general welfare clauses of Article I would give too much power to Congress. The Republicans were concerned with how the federal government would use this power.

Problem solving

How well do you understand Jefferson's concern?

Suppose the members of your student government had the power to make whatever rules for your school they thought were "necessary and proper" for your "general welfare."

- Who would be in a position to decide what was "necessary and proper"?

- Who would decide what the "general welfare" was?

- What limitations would there be on the student government's powers?

Disagreements over the Bank of the United States

Hamilton and Jefferson disagreed about the policies of the new government. They argued whether to create a national bank. Hamilton was the Secretary of the Treasury. He wanted to do things that would strengthen the nation's economy and solve the problem of the national and state debts. In 1790, Hamilton asked Congress to establish a Bank of the United States.

The Bank would help in collecting taxes, borrowing money, and regulating trade.

Hamilton told President Washington that the necessary and proper clause of the Constitution gave the federal government the power to create the Bank of the United States. He argued that such a bank was a "necessary and proper" way for the government to act regarding taxes and trade.

Thomas Jefferson disagreed. He said the necessary and proper clause should be interpreted to allow the federal government to do only those things which were "absolutely necessary."

After listening to both arguments, President Washington signed the bill establishing the Bank of the United States. By doing so, he increased the power of the federal government. Not everyone agreed with Washington's decision. People began to take sides on whether the government had acted properly according to the guidelines set down in the Constitution.

Disagreements over foreign affairs

Foreign affairs was another area of disagreement. The Federalists, led by Hamilton, believed that the United States should have a close relationship with Great Britain. Most Americans or their families had come from Britain. Many of them favored continued trade with that nation.

Jefferson and his followers wanted a close relationship with France. During the American Revolution, France had supported the colonies. The disagreement between the Federalists and the Republicans became stronger in 1793 when France and Great Britain went to war.

Who are the Federalists and who are the Republicans in this picture?

Washington's warning

Washington thought that it would be harmful to the United States if the nation sided with either Great Britain or France. So he declared that the American government would be neutral and not take sides in the war. When Washington left the presidency, he warned the new nation against entering into any permanent agreements with a foreign government.

Washington also warned the American people about the harmful effects of political parties. It was already too late. By 1796, when John Adams, a Federalist, was elected as President, there was great hostility between the two parties. This was the beginning of the two-party system in American politics.

Political parties today

Political parties are active today on local, state, and national levels. Despite the fears of the Framers, they are an important part of the political system today. The following are some of the ways political parties may be useful.

- Political parties give people a way to join with others of similar interests to try and influence their government.

- People, working through their parties, can nominate candidates for public office, raise money for their candidates, and encourage people to vote for them.

- Political parties can and do get many people involved in the governmental process.

- Political parties give people a choice of candidates and programs.

- The political party that is not in power can debate and criticize the party in power.

Reviewing and using the lesson

1. Why might political parties be a special problem to a new government? Are political parties seen as such a problem today?

2. Explain why Jefferson distrusted the necessary and proper clause of the Constitution. Do you agree with Jefferson's position? Why or why not?

3. Which political party today is most like the Federalists? Which party is most like the Republicans? Explain your position.

4. Do political parties today argue about the same issues that followers of Hamilton and Jefferson argued about? Explain.

Who decides what the Constitution means?

Purpose of Lesson

Even in our nation's earliest years, people such as Hamilton and Jefferson disagreed about exactly what the Constitution meant. Who should decide which interpretation of the Constitution is correct? For example, who should be able to say whether establishing a national bank was allowed under the necessary and proper clause?

This lesson explains how the Supreme Court established its power to make such decisions. This is called the power of judi-cial review. When you have completed this lesson, you should be able to explain what is meant by judicial review. You should also be able to discuss how the Supreme Court established its power of judicial review in one of the most important cases in our nation's history.

Terms to know

judicial review
null and void
opinion
Marbury v. Madison

How does the Supreme Court reach a decision?

Judicial review

Judicial review is the power of the courts to decide whether laws and actions of the government are allowed under the Constitution. When a court decides they are not allowed, it orders that the law or action be considered **null and void**. A law that is null and void may not be enforced.

Judicial review over state governments

The Framers wanted to be sure the states had to obey the laws of the federal government. That is why they wrote in Article VI that the Constitution and the federal laws are the "supreme law of the land." If state laws conflict with those of the federal government, the Supreme Court can order that the state laws not be enforced.

The Supreme Court first used its power of judicial review over state governments in 1796. After the Revolution, the United States had signed a peace treaty with Great Britain. This treaty said that Americans would pay all debts they owed to British citizens. However, Virginia passed a law that cancelled all debts owed by its citizens to the British. Since this law violated the peace treaty, the Supreme Court ruled that the law could not be enforced. Citizens of Virginia would have to pay their debts.

Judicial review over acts of Congress

The Framers clearly meant that the Supreme Court should have the power of judicial review over acts of state governments. However, the Constitution does not clearly say whether the Supreme Court has the power of judicial review over the legislative and executive branches of the federal government.

The Supreme Court established its power of judicial review over the other branches of the federal government in one of the most famous cases in our history. This case, *Marbury v. Madison*, was decided in 1803. We will look at it in some detail and see how the Supreme Court declared an act of Congress unconstitutional.

<u>Marbury</u> v. <u>Madison</u>

During the last few weeks that John Adams was President, he appointed a number of Federalists to office. Among others, he appointed William Marbury to be a justice of the peace for the District of Columbia. However, some of the papers making these last-minute appointments were not actually delivered. Thomas Jefferson, a Republican, then became President. Jefferson ordered his Secretary of State, James Madison, not to deliver these remaining appointments.

Why did Marbury bring his case
to the Supreme Court?

Marbury thought he had the right to the job he had been given by President Adams. He discovered that the Judiciary Act of 1789 gave the Supreme Court the power to order Madison to give him the job. So Marbury took his case directly to the Supreme Court as he had a right to do under the Judiciary Act.

Chief Justice John Marshall wrote the **opinion** for the Supreme Court. The Court ruled that Marbury did have a right to his job. However, the Court decided that the part of the Judiciary Act which gave Marbury the right to bring his case directly to the Supreme Court was unconstitutional. The Constitution clearly limits the cases which can go directly to the Supreme Court without having been heard first in a lower court. Marbury's case did not fit within these limits.

In the Judiciary Act, Congress had given Marbury the right to bring his case directly to the Supreme Court. By doing this, Congress had changed the Constitution. Congress does not have the right to change the Constitution. So, the Supreme court ruled that the part of the Judiciary Act which increased the Court's power was unconstitutional.

By declaring part of a law passed by Congress unconstitutional, the Supreme Court **assumed** the power of judicial review over the legislative and executive branches. Justice Marshall argued that the people of this nation had adopted the Constitution as the supreme law of the land and consented to be governed by its rules. These rules include important limitations upon the powers of Congress. When Congress violates those limitations, it has violated the will of the people.

Marshall said if the Supreme Court could not strike down such acts, there would be no effective way to enforce the constitutional limits on the powers of Congress. Its powers would be unlimited, and we would no longer have a constitutional government. Since the decision of *Marbury v. Madison*, the Supreme Court has exercised the power of judicial review over the federal government.

What was the importance of Marshall's opinion in the *Marbury v. Madison* case?

Reviewing and using the lesson

1. What is judicial review?

2. If judicial review had not been established, how could disagreements over the meaning of the Constitution have been decided?

3. How does judicial review protect the rights of the minority?

4. Some people argue that judicial review allows the courts to overrule the will of the people as expressed through their legislatures. Do you agree? Why or why not?

5. If there were no power of judicial review, how could the people be sure members of government obeyed the limitations set upon their powers by the Constitution?

How does the Supreme Court interpret the Constitution?

Purpose of Lesson

What is the best way to decide what the Constitution means? Some parts of the Constitution are clear and easy to understand; others are much more difficult. For example, what do the terms "general welfare," "necessary and proper," and "due process of law" mean?

This lesson discusses the most common approaches the Supreme Court has used to decide what the Constitution means. When you have completed the lesson, you should be able to describe these approaches. You should also be able to give the arguments in favor of or against each of these methods.

Difficulties of interpretation

Deciding what the Constitution means has been a continuous process throughout our history. Even the justices of the Supreme Court sometimes disagree about the best method of interpreting the Constitution. That is one of the reasons some important Court decisions have been made by a five-to-four vote of the justices.

Problem solving

How would you decide?

The language in many parts of the Constitution can be interpreted in more than one way. The Fourth Amendment protects citizens against "unreasonable searches and seizures." If you were a member of the Supreme Court, how would you decide what is "unreasonable"?

- Would you look up the words in a dictionary to decide what they mean?

- Would you try to think how the Framers would have decided the case?

- Would you take into consideration such ideas as basic rights and limited government?

- Would you be influenced by historical, political, and social changes that have occurred since the Constitution was written?

How much importance would you give to previous Court rulings on this issue?

Which method of constitutional interpretation is illustrated by each of these pictures?

How does the Court decide what the Constitution means?

There are three basic methods the Supreme Court has used when it considers a case. Each of these approaches has its advantages and disadvantages.

1. **The meaning of the language of the Constitution.** With this method, the justices study what the words meant at the time they were written. The difficulty is that even at the Philadelphia Convention there was disagreement over the meaning of some words. Also, people today do not agree with some of the ideas of the 18th century such as treating black people as personal property.

2. **The intention of the Framers.** This approach says the justices should base their decisions on how the Framers would

have decided. It is the method most faithful to the basic ideas in the Constitution. However, it is extremely difficult, if not impossible, to find out what the Framers really intended on some issues. There were differences of opinion among the Framers. Which of these men's ideas should be followed? This method of interpretation also gives no guidelines about situations that did not exist when the Constitution was written.

3. **Basic values and principles.** The Constitution contains basic ideas such as the responsibility of the government to promote the general welfare and protect the rights of the people. Some people argue that the justices should base their decisions on such principles taking into account the changes that have occurred in our history and social values. Opponents of this method say it gives the justices too much freedom to decide cases according to their own political and personal ideas.

In deciding a case, the Supreme Court justices are influenced by a number of things. They consider the language and intention of the Framers as well as the principles of the Constitution itself. They pay attention to the previous decisions of the Court. They are aware of the current political, social, and economic situation. Finally, the justices are influenced, as is everyone, by their own personal beliefs.

The Supreme Court's decisions often raise much controversy — especially when the Court has attempted to define and protect certain basic rights. In the next unit, we will look at some of these controversies.

Reviewing and using the lesson

1. How can the Supreme Court decide cases involving subjects, such as wiretapping, which did not exist when the Constitution was written?

2. Would you agree with the following statement by Charles Evans Hughes who was a Chief Justice of the Supreme Court, "We are under a Constitution, but the Constitution is what the judges say it is"? Why or why not?

3. Would you agree with the following statement by Justice Felix Frankfurter, "As a member of this court I am not justified in writing my opinions into the Constitution, no matter how deeply I may cherish them." Why or why not?

Unit Five: How does the Constitution protect our basic rights?

Purpose of Unit Five

You have learned that one of the most important purposes of the government established by the Founders was to protect the basic rights of the people. The addition of the Bill of Rights to the Constitution was intended to achieve that purpose.

But even adding the Bill of Rights did not guarantee that all people would have the rights we value. In this unit, you will learn about five fundamental rights and how they have been extended to many people who were denied them in the past.

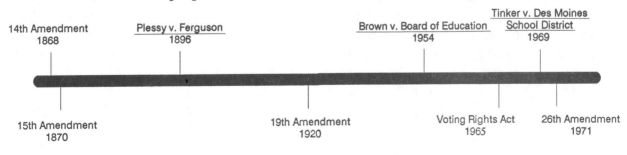

14th Amendment
1868

Plessy v. Ferguson
1896

Brown v. Board of Education
1954

Tinker v. Des Moines
School District
1969

15th Amendment
1870

19th Amendment
1920

Voting Rights Act
1965

26th Amendment
1971

How does the Constitution protect freedom of expression?

Purpose of Lesson

In this lesson, you will learn why the Founders considered freedom of expression so important. You will also learn why it is important to you as an individual and to the preservation and improvement of our constitutional democracy. When you have completed this lesson, you should be able to explain the importance of freedom of expression. You should also be able to describe situations in which it might be reasonable and fair to place limitations on this freedom.

Terms to know
abridging
petition
"redress of grievances"
freedom of expression

What is freedom of expression?

"...secure the blessings of liberty to ourselves and our posterity [future generations]...." *Preamble of the Constitution*

One of the purposes of government is to protect our liberty. What does "liberty" mean? When you answer this question you are likely to think of some of the freedoms guaranteed by the First Amendment to the Constitution. It is probably the best-known amendment to the Constitution. Here is what one section of it says:

Congress shall make no law... **abridging** [limiting] the freedom of speech, or of the press; or the right of the people peaceably to assemble, and to **petition** [ask] the government for a **redress of grievances** [to correct wrongs].

Freedom of speech, freedom of the press, freedom of assembly, and freedom of petition are all part of the right to **freedom of expression** protected by the First Amendment. It is important to understand that this Amendment limits the powers of Congress. It prevents Congress from placing unreasonable and unfair limits on freedom of expression. That is why the Amendment begins with the phrase, "Congress shall make no law...."

Why was freedom of expression so important to the Founders?

The way the First Amendment was written makes it clear that the Founders believed freedom of expression was very important. They knew this right had to be protected from government interference. Governments had often limited freedom of expression to try to stop people from criticizing their actions. Some of the historical examples the Founders knew about were:

- **Massachusetts Colony - 1660.** Mary Dyer taught that all men and women were equal before God and that slavery, war, and capital punishment were evil.

She was hanged by the Puritans because her ideas were different from many of theirs.

- **Virginia Colony - 1682.** John Buckner was accused of printing the laws without permission of the governor. The governor decided to ban all printing presses in the colony. He said, "Printing has encouraged [the people] to learn and even criticize the best governments. God keep us from free schools and printing."

- **New York Colony - 1735.** John Peter Zenger, a newspaperman, wrote strong criticisms about government dishonesty and incompetence. Zenger was arrested for his statements. After a long trial, he was released because the jury decided that what he had said about the government was true.

Why do you think freedom of the press is an important right?

What are some of the benefits of freedom of expression?

The Founders knew about these and many other events in history where people had been unfairly deprived of their right to freedom of expression. They also believed in natural rights and representative democracy. They believed that the right to hold and express one's beliefs was essential to being a responsible citizen. The following are some of the arguments for the importance of this right.

1. **Individual development and human dignity.** It is important to your growth as a person to have the right to present your ideas and to consider other points of view. Your dignity as a person should be respected by allowing you the freedom to say what you think and to hear what others think.

2. **Advancement of knowledge.** It is easier for new discoveries to be made when ideas can be discussed freely. Even if you disagree with someone, that person may say something that helps you test your knowledge and increase your understanding.

3. **The maintenance of representative democracy.** Individual citizens participate in running our country through their power to vote for government officials and make choices about government policies. In order to make wise choices, you need to have good information. Free expression does not guarantee complete or accurate information, but it increases the chances of getting such information.

4. **Peaceful social change.** Free speech allows you to try to influence public opinion by persuasion without feeling you have to resort to violence to make changes. Also, if you have the opportunity to express your opinions freely, you may be more willing to accept government decisions, even ones you do not agree with.

When should freedom of expression be limited?

Many people believe that freedom of expression is absolutely necessary for the protection of all of our individual freedoms. Does this mean there are no limits to freedom of expression? For example, should you have the right to yell "Fire!" in a crowded theater, even when there is no fire, just to terrify people? Why should this not be allowed as free speech?

Other situations are more complicated. What if you want to convince other people that we should change our way of government? Should the government be able to keep you from doing so just because it doesn't like your ideas? What if you are part of an unpopular group that wants to have a public demonstration? Should the government be able to stop you by saying that your demonstration **may** cause a riot?

Over the years, the courts in our country have developed guidelines to use in limiting freedom of expression. These guidelines are used to decide when the right to free expression interferes with other important rights and interests. For example, suppose your right to freedom of expression in a particular situation is dangerous to public safety, national security, or some other important interest. If the danger is great enough, the courts sometimes allow freedom of expression to be limited.

When have you exercised your right to freedom of speech?

Also, one person's right to freedom of speech may conflict with someone else's right to free speech. If two people attempt to talk at the same time, neither can be heard. For this reason, we accept limitations that are intended to protect everyone's right to speak.

When might it be necessary to limit freedom of expression?

Freedom of expression in the schools

What should be a student's right to freedom of expression in the schools? When should students' freedom of expression be limited? The following are two important Supreme Court cases that deal with these questions.

Tinker v. Des Moines School District (1969)

This case involved a few high school students who wore black armbands to school. They were protesting American involvement in the Vietnam War. The school principal told the students to remove the armbands. They refused and were then suspended from school until they agreed to come back without the armbands. Their parents took the case to court. They argued that the school administration was depriving the students of their right to freedom of expression.

The school administration argued that they were justified in suspending the students. They said the suspension had been necessary to prevent any school disturbance that might have been caused by the wearing of the armbands.

The Supreme Court ruled that the school administration's action was an unnecessary limitation on freedom of expression. The Court's guideline was that a school cannot limit a student's right to freedom of expression unless the student's exercise of that right disrupts the educational process. In this case, the Court said, there was "no evidence whatever of...interference...with the school's work or of collision with the rights of other students to be secure and to be let alone."

Justice Abe Fortas wrote the opinion for the Court. He said, "Any word spoken, in class, in the lunchroom or on the campus, that deviates from the views of another person, may start an argument or cause a disturbance. But our Constitution says we must take this risk...and our history says that it is this sort of hazardous freedom — this kind of openness — that is the basis of our national strength and of the independence...of Americans...."

This opinion of the Supreme Court clearly confirms the Founders' belief in the importance of freedom of expression. The Court said that students do not give up their "constitutional rights to freedom of speech or expression at the schoolhouse gate." Freedom of expression should be protected unless it clearly violates other important rights and interests such as the "school's work or the right of students to be secure and to be let alone."

How might the *Tinker* case be applied to this illustration?

Problem solving

Balancing rights and interests

The following case involves a situation in which students' rights to freedom of expression must be balanced against other important rights and interests. Your class should be divided into groups of about five students each to complete this exercise. Each group should read the case and answer the questions which follow it. Then each group should share its answers with the class for further discussion.

Hazelwood School District v. Kuhlmeier (1988)

A high school newspaper was written in the school's journalism class. One issue of the paper contained an article about teenage pregnancy. The principal thought that the story was not appropriate for younger students in the school. The paper also contained another story in which a student wrote about divorce and made negative remarks about her father. The principal said that the newspaper had not given the father a chance to respond to his daughter's remarks. He ordered both stories to be removed from the paper before it was printed and distributed.

1. What are the conflicting rights and interests in this case?

2. In what ways is this case similar to the *Tinker* case? In what ways is it different?

3. If you used the guideline from the *Tinker* case to decide this case, what decision would you make? Explain your reasoning.

4. What other guidelines might be used in deciding this case? Explain them.

5. How would you decide this case?

Reviewing and using the lesson

1. Restate in your own words the sections of the First Amendment that deal with freedom of expression.

2. Reread the four benefits of free expression described in the lesson. Choose the one that you think is most important. Briefly explain your choice, using a real or imaginary example to support your explanation.

3. Under what conditions do you think public school principals should have the right to censor (restrict) school-sponsored newspapers? Explain your answer.

4. A group dedicated to the belief that white people are superior to other races is planning a public meeting. Members of another organization which represents a minority group, have said that if this meeting is held, they will break it up. There is the possibility of a violent clash between the two groups. Should the government prohibit the group from meeting in public? Explain your answer.

How does the Constitution protect freedom of religion?

Purpose of Lesson

This lesson will explain why the Founders thought religious freedom was so important. It will also discuss the difference between religious beliefs and religious practices, and explain why some limits have been placed on religious practices. Finally, the lesson will introduce you to questions about the relationship between religion and education which the Supreme Court has had to consider. It will also discuss the guidelines the Court has followed in these cases.

When you have completed the lesson, you should be able to explain the importance of freedom of religion and describe situations in which it may be limited. You should also be able to explain the present position of the Supreme Court on the relationship between freedom of religion and the schools.

Terms to know

establishment clause
free exercise clause
Lemon test
parochial school

Why did the Founders think freedom of religion was important?

Read the First Amendment. You will see that the very first clauses say, "Congress shall make no law respecting an establishment of religion, or prohibiting the free exercise thereof;..." These clauses show the importance of freedom of religion to the Framers.

Most of the early colonists were Protestant Christians. Few of the early English colonies in North America allowed religious freedom. In several colonies, one religious group dominated the colony, insisting that everyone conform to its ideas. People who disagreed were often persecuted, and sometimes they were forced to leave. Roger Williams, for example, left the Massachusetts Bay colony with a group of his followers and founded Rhode Island.

Was freedom of religion always guaranteed in America?

By the end of the colonial period, however, there were more people who practiced different religious beliefs. Many had become more tolerant (accepting) of religious differences. Groups such as Quakers, Baptists, Catholics, and others made demands for religious freedom.

Many of the Founders held fundamental beliefs that supported tolerance. Perhaps the most important of these beliefs was that people have certain natural rights simply because they are human beings. Philosophers like John Locke argued that society should allow people to live the way their moral principles, guided by the Bible, tell them is right. The best government, therefore, was the one that interfered as little as possible with personal beliefs, including religious beliefs.

In addition, men like Thomas Jefferson and James Madison were greatly concerned about the dangers of religious intolerance (prejudice). They were well aware that throughout history, religious intolerance had often led to conflict and to the violation of individual rights. They thought religious intolerance was a danger to the community and harmful to religion.

Most of the Founders were religious. They believed that religion was essential to develop the kind of character citizens in a free society need to remain free. At the same time, they believed strongly that everyone has a right to his or her own religious beliefs. For example, George Washington believed that without the influence of religion, people would not behave in moral ways. However, he was against the use of taxes in Virginia to support religious instruction for students.

The protections of religious freedom the Framers placed in the First Amendment demonstrate their belief that the government should not interfere with religion.

Conflicts over freedom of religion

Under the Constitution, conflicts over freedom of religion have focused on the following issues:

- **The establishment of religion.** These conflicts have been about whether the government should be allowed to provide any support at all for religion. Questions about government support of religion are dealt with under the clause of the First Amendment that says that "Congress shall make no law...regarding the establishment of religion...." This clause sets forth the idea that in the United States, the government is to be separated from religion. Sometimes this is called the principle of the "separation of church and state." Exactly what this means is not clear and is a continuing source of conflict. For example, does this mean that government may not be involved in any way with religion?

- **The free exercise of religion.** In addition to forbidding the government from establishing religion, the First Amendment says the government shall make no law prohibiting the free exercise of religion. This means that your right to believe as you wish and, in most cases, practice those beliefs, is protected. This idea is also included in Article VI of the Constitution, which says that no religious test shall ever be required as a qualification for any federal government office.

As you have learned, the First Amendment originally applied only to the federal government. Many states had laws that in some way limited religious freedom. However, in the 1940s the Supreme Court ruled that the First Amendment applies also to state governments. The case involved freedom of belief.

As late as 1961, Maryland had a law requiring anyone who wanted a job in the state government to swear to a belief in God. The law was challenged. The Supreme Court ruled that the law was unconstitutional because it violated the freedom of religious belief guaranteed by the First Amendment. This decision means that each person has an absolute right to hold any or no religious belief. **Freedom of belief** is an unalienable right that cannot be interfered with by the government in any way.

The Supreme Court has ruled, however, that in some situations the government can make laws limiting your right to **practice your beliefs**. For example, religious practices may be limited if they are contrary to public morals, endanger health, or in other ways harm the common welfare. Supreme Court decisions have said that religious practices involving polygamy (being married to more than one person at the same time) or handling rattlesnakes may be forbidden without violating constitutional rights. Children may be required to be vaccinated against diseases before being admitted to public school, even if this requirement violates their religious beliefs.

Why should the government have the right to require
students to be vaccinated if this is against their religious beliefs?

Conflicts between the establishment and the free exercise clauses

Sometimes the free exercise and establishment clauses come into conflict. For example, if the government pays for prison chaplains, it is supporting religion. On the other hand, to prohibit the government from doing this would interfere with the right of prisoners to practice their religion.

Conflicts like these over the relationship between government and religion have caused a number of important cases to be brought before the Supreme Court for settlement. Some of the most controversial cases have dealt with religion and the schools. In each case, the Supreme Court has had the task of deciding how the freedom of religion clauses of the First Amendment should be interpreted.

Should public schools be allowed to set aside time for prayer by students?

Should the government be allowed to support religious education?

At the time the Constitution was written, public schools as we know them did not exist. Children who attended school usually received a great deal of religious training. In fact, their parents wanted the schools to give them religious instruction.

During the 20th century, however, there has been growing disagreement about whether religious teaching should be supported in public schools. In the past 60 years especially, the Supreme Court has heard many cases dealing with this subject. Some of the questions the Court has tried to answer are:

1. Should tax money be used to support parochial schools?

2. Should public schools be allowed to provide certain periods of time during the day when students can attend special classes to receive religious instruction from their own minister, priest, or rabbi?

3. Should public schools be allowed to require students to take part in prayers or the reading of the Bible during regular school hours?

In a 1971 case, Chief Justice Warren E. Burger developed guidelines to be used in deciding if a law involving religion in the schools violated the First Amendment to the Constitution. These guidelines are known as the **Lemon test** because they were written in a case called *Lemon v. Kurtzman* (1971). The three guidelines the law must satisfy to be declared constitutional are:

1. The primary purpose of a law must not be religious. It must have some other purpose, such as furthering education.

2. The primary effect of the law must not be to advance (support) or inhibit (restrict) religion.

3. The law must not create an excessive government entanglement with religion.

Problem solving

Religion and the schools

Use the Lemon test to decide if you think the laws and actions described below should be declared unconstitutional. Be prepared to explain your decision to the class.

1. Your state passes a law allowing your public school principal to post a copy of the Ten Commandments in every classroom.

2. Your state passes a law that gives parents who send their children to parochial schools a tax deduction for tuition, transportation, and educational materials.

3. Your state allows your public school's algebra teacher to spend part of the class day at a church school, giving instruction to students having difficulty with math.

4. A group of students at your public school requests permission to use an empty classroom after regular school hours for a voluntary prayer meeting. The principal refuses to make the classroom available to them.

Reviewing and using the lesson

1. Some religious groups have suggested adding an amendment to the Constitution permitting voluntary prayer in public schools. Would you support such an amendment? Why or why not?

2. Should public schools be permitted to close for Christmas? Why or why not?

3. How would the United States be different today if we had an official national religion? What changes would be good ones? What changes would be bad ones? Explain your answers.

How has the right to vote expanded since the Constitution was adopted?

Purpose of Lesson

The Constitution originally left it up to the state governments to decide who should have the right to vote. In the early years of our nation, the states limited the right to vote to white men who owned property. In 1789, white males who did not own property, members of certain religious groups, free blacks, Native Americans, slaves, and women were not allowed to vote.

In this lesson, we will look at how the right to vote has been expanded in the last two hundred years to achieve a basic ideal of our representative democracy—the constitutional right of all adult citizens to vote.

When you have completed this lesson, you should be able to explain how voting rights were extended by changes in state voting laws, by amendments to the Constitution, by acts of Congress, and by decisions of the Supreme Court.

Terms to know

suffrage
poll tax
literacy test
grandfather clause
register

Which of the people in this picture would have been eligible to vote in the federal election of 1788?

Extending the right to vote to all white males

The colonial limits on who could vote were also used during the early years of the new nation. Many colonies only gave the right to vote to white men who owned property and who belonged to a particular religious group.

After the Revolution, an increasing number of people objected to these limits on voting rights. States began to eliminate property and religious restrictions. In addition, new states joining the Union placed fewer limitations on **suffrage** (the right to vote). In the early 1800s, for example, six new western states gave the vote to all white males. By the time of the election of Andrew Jackson as President in 1828, the process of giving voting rights to more people was well on its way.

Although the states took many steps before the Civil War to extend suffrage, change was not easy. For example, as late as 1842 in Rhode Island, only men with property—less than half of the adult males—were allowed to vote. This situation caused an armed rebellion led by Thomas Dorr, a Providence lawyer, whose story is told below. The rebellion failed but the following year a new state constitution was adopted that gave voting rights to all male citizens who paid a tax of at least one dollar a year. Yet a large part of the population—including blacks and women—still could not vote.

Problem solving

Rebellion over voting rights — right or wrong?

Pretend you are the publisher of a newspaper in 1842. One of your reporters has written the following news story about Dorr's Rebellion. Now you are to write an editorial supporting or attacking Dorr. Which position will you take? Think about what you have learned about the social compact and representative democracy in making your decision.

Providence, R.I., May, 1842 — Thomas W. Dorr, leader of the rebel "People's Government," has fled Rhode Island after the state militia disbanded his group. Dorr and his followers had established a separate government in protest against the voting laws of Rhode Island. The state's constitution says that only property owners and their oldest sons may vote. The rebels argue that all white males should have the right to vote.

Dorr and his followers held a convention in Providence at which Dorr was elected governor under a "People's Constitution." Members of the Dorr group were declared rebels by the state, which began to imprison some of Dorr's followers. Outraged, Dorr led a band of his men in an attack on the arsenal at Providence. Martial law was imposed, and the state militia was called to put down the rebellion.

The President of the United States, John Tyler, said he would not support the Dorr group but instead would call out federal troops to aid the "legitimate" government of Rhode Island.

Extending the right to vote to black males

Although many blacks fought in the Revolutionary War, the Americans' newly-won rights were not given to them. For example, in 1860, only 6 of the 34 states allowed free blacks to vote. The 14th and 15th Amendments to the Constitution, passed after the Civil War, gave full citizenship to blacks and guaranteed the right to vote regardless "of race, color, or previous condition of servitude." But much remained to be done to make the rights guaranteed by these amendments a reality.

Many people in the southern states did not want blacks to vote or hold office. Some state governments passed laws that made it impossible for blacks to vote. **Poll taxes, literacy tests,** and **grandfather clauses** were three ways the states kept blacks from voting.

Problem solving

How were blacks kept from voting?

Copy the chart below onto a piece of paper. Look up in the Glossary the three terms in the first column. Write a definition in the second column. Then think about what you have learned about slavery and voting rights in the 1800s. In the third column, explain how each law kept black people from voting.

Law	Definition	Result
Poll tax		
Literacy test		
Grandfather clause		

How would you caption this picture?

Removing state barriers to voting

It was not until recently in our history that actions were finally taken to extend voting rights to most blacks. The Twenty-Fourth Amendment to the Constitution (1964) denied states the right to require poll taxes in federal elections. In 1966, states were denied the right to require poll taxes in state elections in the case of *Harper v. Virginia Board of Education*. Congress passed the Voting Rights Act in 1965. It denied states the right to require literacy tests before allowing people to vote. It also gave the federal government the authority to register voters in areas where blacks were prevented from voting.

Extending the right to vote to women

In 1848, a convention was held at Seneca Falls, New York, which launched a national movement by women to win the right to vote. Although suffrage for women had many supporters among men, the battle was difficult. When the Fifteenth Amendment (1870) gave black males the right to vote, women worked hard to gain the same right. However, at that time many people thought a woman's place was in the home and not in politics. This idea made it harder for women to achieve their goal.

Why was it so difficult for women to win the right to vote?

109

In 1875, the Supreme Court made a decision that denied women a constitutional protection of the right to vote. This was in the case of *Minor v. Happersett*. The Fourteenth Amendment says, "No state shall make or enforce any law which shall abridge the privileges or immunities of citizens of the United States." Women had argued that since they were citizens, this amendment meant that the states could not make laws denying them the right to vote. The Court disagreed. It said that being a citizen does not guarantee a person the right to vote.

In 1876, Susan B. Anthony led a delegation of women to the Philadelphia Centennial Celebration of the Declaration of Independence. These women protested their lack of suffrage by reading the Women's Declaration of Rights.

Change was slow. The territory of Wyoming had allowed women to vote before 1890. But by 1900, only Colorado, Utah, and Idaho had followed Wyoming's lead.

It was not until 1912 that the movement to give women the right to vote gained national recognition. Presidential candidate Theodore Roosevelt's Bull Moose Progressive Party supported women's suffrage. In 1920, the Nineteenth Amendment to the Constitution was ratified. One hundred thirty years after the Constitution was signed, women had gained the right to vote.

Extending the right to vote to eighteen-year-olds

In the 1950s, Senator Jennings Randolph of West Virginia introduced an amendment to lower the age requirement on voting from twenty-one to eighteen. Progress was slow until the Vietnam War. Thousands of young men were drafted to fight in Vietnam. However, they were not able to vote in the elections that chose the members of government responsible for deciding America's role in that war.

Congress passed a law in 1970 lowering the voting age to eighteen. But the Supreme Court ruled that Congress could only regulate the age of voters in federal elections, not in state elections. At that time, only four states allowed eighteen-year-olds to vote. Within six months of the Supreme Court's decision, steps were taken to amend the Constitution so that suffrage would be extended to eighteen-year-olds in both state and federal elections.

In 1971, the Twenty-Sixth Amendment was added to the Constitution. This amendment says that anyone eighteen years old or older cannot be denied the right to vote because of age.

Voting requirements today

The states, although limited by the Constitution and the federal Voting Rights Act, still make some decisions regarding voting rights. For example, all states have laws saying only citizens have the right to vote, although the Constitution does not require this. Every state requires that persons must live in the state for a period of time before they can vote, and all states except North Dakota require citizens to **register** in order to vote.

The right to vote in our democracy is a closely guarded right. Yet it is a right that has taken many citizens a long time and much hard work to achieve.

How was the right to vote extended to each of the groups in this picture?

Reviewing and using the lesson

1. List the restrictions on voting rights that have kept various groups from voting.

2. List the ways in which various groups have won the right to vote.

3. Why do you think it took so long for women to win suffrage?

4. Why do you think that action by the federal government was necessary to gain voting rights for some groups of people?

5. What restrictions, if any, do you think states should be able to place on voting rights? Explain your position.

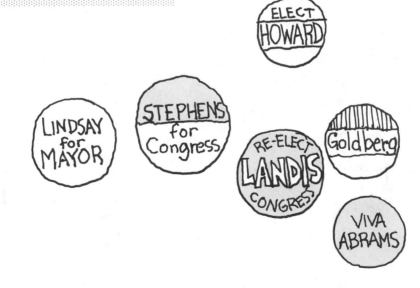

What is the right to equal protection of the laws?

Purpose of Lesson

In this lesson you will be introduced to one of the most important parts of the Fourteenth Amendment to the Constitution—the equal protection clause. When you have completed this lesson, you should be able to explain its purpose and describe the changes in how it has been interpreted by the Supreme Court. You should also be able to describe some of the steps that have been taken to end unfair discrimination in our nation.

Terms to know

Thirteenth Amendment
Fourteenth Amendment
equal protection clause
jurisdiction
"Jim Crow laws"
"separate but equal"
segregation

Problem solving

What is unfair discrimination?

Do you think the following situations are examples of unfair discrimination? Why or why not?

1. Your state has a law that says that all students of your race must go to separate schools from the other students in your community.

2. Your city has a regulation that says your family cannot live in some sections of town because of your religious beliefs.

3. Your state has a law that says you cannot marry someone of a different race.

4. Your city fire department will not hire women as firefighters.

5. You and a friend of the opposite sex work for the state at the same jobs. Yet you are paid much less than your friend.

Do you think people should receive equal pay for the same work?

The Fourteenth Amendment and equal protection of the laws

The **Thirteenth Amendment** was added to the Constitution in 1865 after the Civil War. It abolished slavery in the United States, but it did not end prejudice against black people. This prejudice could easily be seen in state laws in the South that discriminated against black people in many different ways. For example, state and local laws required that public facilities such as restrooms, theaters, and parks have separate areas for blacks and whites.

To prevent state governments from discriminating against blacks, Congress adopted the **Fourteenth Amendment** in 1868. The **equal protection clause** of that amendment is the most important constitutional protection of people against unfair discrimination by state and local governments. In recent years the Supreme Court has used it to eliminate governmental discrimination and to try to correct the effects of past discrimination.

The equal protection clause says that "No State shall... deny to any person within its **jurisdiction** [the territory it controls] the equal protection of the laws." At the time it was ratified, this clause was intended to prevent discrimination against blacks and guarantee them the rights that go along with citizenship.

The Fourteenth Amendment did not by itself prevent discrimination, however. A number of state governments passed laws requiring blacks to go to separate schools and to use separate public facilities. These laws came to be called **"Jim Crow laws."** The states said these laws did not violate the equal protection clause because the separate schools and facilities provided for blacks were equal to those provided for whites. The Supreme Court considered this argument in two famous cases.

The Supreme Court and equal protection

The state of Louisiana had passed a law requiring railroad companies to provide **separate but equal** cars for white and black passengers. A group of black leaders decided to challenge the law. A black man named Homer Plessy bought a railroad ticket and sat in a car set aside for whites. He was arrested when he refused to ride in the car for blacks. Plessy was convicted in the state court. He took his case to the United States Supreme Court, arguing that the Louisiana law violated the equal protection clause.

Plessy lost his case. The Supreme Court said that separating the races did not mean one race was inferior to the other. Since the law required that the facilities be equal, the Court said there was no discrimination.

The decision in this case, *Plessy v. Ferguson* (1896), allowed states to practice **segregation** (separation of the races) for almost sixty years. Then, in the case of *Brown v. Board of Education* (1954), the Supreme Court changed its interpretation of the equal protection clause.

Linda Brown was a seven-year-old child who lived five blocks from an elementary school. Because Linda was black and the students in that school were white, she was forced to attend a school for black children twenty-one blocks away. Her parents sued the school board of Topeka, Kansas, saying their daughter had been deprived of equal protection of the law.

The Browns' lawyer was Thurgood Marshall, an attorney for the National Association for the Advancement of Colored

People. Marshall later became the first black justice of the Supreme Court. He argued that segregated schools could **not** be equal. This time the Court agreed. It said that placing black children in schools separate from white children denied them the equal protection of the laws guaranteed by the Fourteenth Amendment.

The Court said, "To separate [children]...solely because of their race, [causes] a feeling of inferiority...that may affect their hearts and minds in a way unlikely ever to be undone...."

Ending discrimination

The Court's decision in *Brown v. Board of Education* was the first important step in ending school segregation. But it did not by itself end discrimination. Many states resisted the Court's order to integrate their schools. As late as 1957, the governor of Arkansas tried to stop black students from entering an all-white high school in Little Rock. In response, President Dwight Eisenhower ordered the U.S. Army to go to that city to enforce the law.

Although the *Brown* case was a turning point in the fight against discrimination, it dealt only with segregated schools. In the 1960s, many blacks and whites worked together to end racial discrimination in other areas of society. Through their efforts, laws were passed to prohibit other types of unfair discrimination, including discrimination in housing and employment.

As blacks won these civil rights after years of struggle, other groups began to call for equal protection. Women, disabled persons, older persons, and other groups worked to get laws passed guaranteeing their rights. In response to their efforts, Congress and state legislatures have passed laws prohibiting unfair discrimination against these groups.

What effect do you think school segregation might have had on the students in this picture?

How did the *Brown v. Board of Education* case eventually lead to school integration?

Reviewing and using the lesson

1. When was the 14th Amendment ratified and what was its purpose?

2. What did the Supreme Court decide in the *Plessy v. Ferguson* case? How would this decision affect your life if you were a black student living in 1900? How did the Court explain that this decision offered all citizens equal protection under the law?

3. How did the decision in *Brown v. Board of Education* differ from the Court's earlier ruling in *Plessy v. Ferguson*?

4. How might the Fourteenth Amendment be used to support the rights of women, the disabled, and others who believe they are not receiving equal treatment?

5. Are there times when your right to equal protection of the law might conflict with another person's right to privacy or property? For example, is it fair for a state to require private men's clubs to admit women as members? Explain both sides of this issue.

What is the right to due process and how is it protected?

Purpose of Lesson

Fairness is an important idea to Americans. It is an idea we learn at an early age in our society. We begin to say "But that's not fair!" when we are still very young.

Think of a situation in which you or someone you know was treated unfairly. What was unfair or unjust about the situation? How could this unfairness or injustice have been prevented? In what kinds of situations do you think people should have their right to fair treatment protected by law?

In the last lesson we examined the equal protection clause in the Constitution that deals with unfair discrimination. In this lesson we will look at another clause in the Constitution that is concerned with fairness—the due process clause. This clause is intended to guarantee that the government will not interfere with an individual's right to life, liberty, or property without a good and fair reason.

When you have completed the lesson you should be able to explain in general terms what due process means and particularly how it has been applied to the rights of juveniles who are accused of breaking the law.

Terms to know
due process clause
procedure

The due process clauses

A **due process clause** can be found in two places in the Constitution—in the Fifth Amendment of the Bill of Rights, ratified in 1791, and in the Fourteenth Amendment, ratified in 1868.

The Fifth Amendment and the other amendments that make up the Bill of Rights were designed to protect people from unfair and unreasonable treatment by the **federal** government. The Bill of Rights did not at first protect people from unfair treatment by **state** governments.

The Fifth Amendment says:

No person shall...be deprived of life, liberty, or property, without due process of law;...

The Fourteenth Amendment contains a due process clause that is intended to limit the powers of **state** governments. Over the years, the Supreme Court has interpreted this clause to mean that almost all of the protections in the Bill of Rights apply also to actions of state governments.

The Fourteenth Amendment, Section 1, says:

...nor shall any State deprive any person of life, liberty, or property, without due process of law;...

Compare these two pictures. What effect did the passage of the 14th Amendment have on the way the Bill of Rights is applied?

What is due process of law?

It is impossible to define "due process of law" exactly. The closest meaning is that the right to due process is the right to be treated fairly by government. There are two important ways this meaning is applied.

- Due process means that the **content** of laws that legislatures pass must be fair and reasonable. Congress and the state legislatures cannot pass laws that place unfair or unreasonable limitations on people's rights to life, liberty, or property.

- Due process means that the **procedures**, or methods used to conduct hearings and to apply and enforce the law, must be fair and reasonable. All branches of the federal and state governments must use fair procedures when they are carrying out the responsibilities given to them by the people.

This lesson will deal with the second meaning of due process — that members of all branches of government must use fair procedures when fulfilling their responsibilities. We will concentrate on the rights of persons suspected or accused of crimes. To show the importance of due process, we will examine the procedures followed in a situation that led to a famous Supreme Court case called *In re Gault*. This case concerns the treatment of a juvenile accused of a crime.

Problem solving

What are fair procedures?

Your class should be divided into small groups for the following activities:

1. Read the case that follows.

2. Make a list of the procedures used by government officials in Gerald Gault's case that the group thinks were unfair.

3. Identify the parts of Amendments V and VI of the Bill of Rights that the group thinks should apply to the procedures used in this case.

4. Take and defend a position on how the Supreme Court should have dealt with this case.

Was Gerald Gault treated fairly?

Fifteen-year-old Gerald Gault was already on six months' probation because he had been in the company of another boy who had stolen a wallet from a woman's purse. At about 10 a.m. on June 8, 1964, Gerald and a friend, Ronald Lewis, were arrested by the Sheriff of Gila County. The boys were taken to the county Children's Detention Home. They were accused of telephoning a neighbor of the boys, Mrs. Cook, and saying offensive and obscene things to her. Mrs. Cook had called the sheriff.

The boys were questioned by the superintendent of the detention home, Probation Officer Flagg. The boys admitted making the calls, but each boy blamed the other.

At the time Gerald was picked up, his parents were at work. The sheriff did not leave a notice telling them Gerald was being taken to the detention home. No one from the sheriff's office called the Gaults. When his mother arrived home at about 6 p.m. to find Gerald gone, she sent his older brother to the Lewis's home. The brother learned that Gerald was being held in the detention home. He went home and told his mother, and the two of them went to the detention home. There, Officer Flagg told Mrs. Gault why Jerry was taken there. He said there would be a hearing in juvenile court the next afternoon.

The next day, Officer Flagg told Judge McGhee of the juvenile court that Gerald was under 18 years of age and a juvenile delinquent. Gerald, his mother, his older brother, Officer Flagg, and Judge McGhee were at the hearing. Gerald's father was at work outside the city. Mrs. Cook was not present either.

No one was asked to swear to tell the truth at this hearing. No record was made of what was said. No lawyers were present. At later hearings, Judge McGhee, Mrs. Gault, and Officer Flagg agreed on some things that were said at the first hearing and disagreed about others. They agreed that the judge had asked Gerald about the telephone call. They disagreed about what Gerald answered. His mother remembered that Gerald said he had dialed Mrs. Cook's number and then handed the telephone to Ronald. Officer Flagg said that Gerald had admitted making one insulting remark.

After the first hearing, Gerald was taken back to the detention home. Two or three days later, he was driven home. No explanation was given for why he was kept in the detention home or why he was taken home.

On the day Gerald was driven home, his mother received a note from Officer Flagg. It was on plain paper. It said: "Mrs. Gault, Judge McGhee has set Monday, June 15, 1964, at 11:00 for further hearings on Gerald's delinquency."

On June 15, the Gaults appeared in court before Judge McGhee. Mrs. Cook was not at this hearing either, although Mrs. Gault had asked that she be present. Judge McGhee, who had never spoken with Mrs. Cook, said that she did not have to be there. Again no one was asked to swear to tell the truth and no record was made of this hearing. People at this hearing later disagreed about what happened. Mr. and Mrs. Gault remembered that Gerald again said he had only dialed the number. Gerald did not admit making the remarks. Judge McGhee later said Gerald had admitted making nuisance calls in the past, "silly calls, or funny calls, or something like that."

At this hearing, the probation officer gave the judge a report that was not given to the Gaults. This report said Gerald had made insulting phone calls. The judge ruled that Gerald had broken a section of the Arizona criminal law that said that a person who "in the presence of or hearing of any woman or child...uses vulgar, abusive, or obscene language, is guilty of a misdemeanor." The judge committed Gerald as a juvenile delinquent to the State Industrial School until he reached age 21, unless he was discharged sooner by "due process of law."

If Gerald had been 18, he would have been tried in a regular criminal court. There, the maximum penalty for making "vulgar, abusive, or obscene" calls would have been a $5 to $50 fine or not more than two months' imprisonment.

Mr. and Mrs. Gault filed a petition for Gerald's release from the Industrial School, which was denied. The case was appealed by Gerald's lawyer, Amelia Lewis, and eventually reached the United States Supreme Court. His lawyers argued that the procedure used in Gerald's case had denied him due process under the

Fourteenth Amendment. Attorneys for the state argued that the informal proceedings under the juvenile court system were intended to help juveniles, rather than treat them as regular criminals. They said this system would be undermined if the Court gave young offenders all the specific guarantees in the Bill of Rights.

The rights of the individual versus the rights of society

Problems of due process involve two responsibilities of government that sometimes conflict. These are the government's responsibility to:

- protect the rights of the individual who may have broken the law, and

- protect everyone else from people who break the law and endanger the lives, liberty, or property of others.

Balancing these two responsibilities is a difficult job that members of the government and the courts must face. In spite of this difficulty, the due process protections of the individual against unfair treatment by government is among the most important protections of our constitutional democracy.

What are some of the issues that require our courts to balance the rights of the individual against those of society?

Due process in other situations

This lesson has dealt with due process of law as it applies to the rights of people accused of crimes. However, the right to due process means the right to be treated fairly by all agencies of government, not just the courts and law enforcement agencies. It applies to your local school board hearings, to congressional hearings, and to hearings of the administrative agencies of your state and federal government. Due process of law has been called the "primary and indispensable foundation of individual freedom" because it protects the individual from government wrongdoing.

Reviewing and using the lesson

1. Why do you think the guarantee of due process is so important?

2. Why are the courts given the responsibility to protect due process?

3. Should adults and juveniles be treated alike when they break laws? Explain your answer.

Do you think that juveniles and adults accused of crimes should be treated the same?

Unit Six: What are the responsibilities of citizens?

What responsibilities of citizenship do you see illustrated here? What others can you think of?

Purpose of Unit Six

You have studied the basic ideas of our constitutional democracy. You have learned of our government's responsibility to protect basic rights and promote the common welfare. This unit deals with a question that is of equal or greater importance. What is the role of the citizen?

We will not attempt to answer this question for you. The answer is one you must arrive at yourself. This unit will raise some of the important ideas you should find useful in deciding what your responsibilities are as a citizen.

How can citizens participate?

Purpose of Lesson

In this lesson you will learn about one of the most important rights of citizenship. This is the right to participate in governing our nation. The lesson will discuss the different ways you may participate. It will also suggest those things you should think about in deciding whether or not you should participate.

When you finish the lesson, you should know the difference between a citizen and a non-citizen. You should also be able to support your views on whether and to what extent a citizen should participate in government.

Terms to know

citizen
alien

Who is a citizen?

Anyone who is born in the United States or whose parents are U.S. citizens is a **citizen** of the United States. An **alien** is a person who is not a citizen. Many aliens can become citizens by following certain rules and procedures.

The government protects many rights for anyone who lives in the United States. But citizens have one right aliens do not have. That is the right to vote and be elected to public office. Many people say that citizens also have important responsibilities to their country that aliens do not. We will examine what those responsibilities might be in this lesson.

Problem solving

Examining participation

The Founders believed that the main purposes of government were to protect people's basic rights and promote the common welfare. Almost all citizens have the right to participate in governing our nation. They may choose among many different ways of doing this. Some ways to participate are listed below.

Your class should be divided into small groups. Each group should read the list of ways citizens can participate. Then each group should answer the following questions and share its responses with the class.

1. What are the advantages and disadvantages of each form of participation that is listed?

2. Are all these forms of participation equally important in protecting our basic rights? Why or why not? Which seem the most important?

Ways citizens can participate

- looking for information in newspapers, magazines, and reference materials and judging its accuracy

- voting in local, state, and national elections

- participating in a political discussion

- signing a petition

- trying to persuade someone to vote a certain way

- wearing a button or putting a sticker on the car

- writing letters to elected representatives

- contributing money to a party or candidate

- attending meetings to gain information, discuss issues, or lend support

- campaigning for a candidate

- lobbying for laws that are of special interest

- demonstrating through marches, boycotts, sit-ins, or other forms of protest

- serving as a juror

- running for office

- holding public office

- serving the country through military or other service

- disobeying laws and taking the consequences to demonstrate that a law or policy is unjust

How does this picture illustrate citizen responsibility?

Should citizens participate?

Many citizens do not participate in our government. They don't vote or participate in most of the other ways you have just discussed. Some people, however, believe that citizens have a responsibility to participate.

Deciding whether to participate and how much time to spend participating is important. To make good decisions, you must think about several things. Some of these are:

- the purpose of our government

- how important your rights are to you

- how satisfied you are with the way the government is working

An example may help. Imagine that you have hired a company to repair your bicycle. Before you hired them, you would want to be sure they could repair bicycles. Then you would want to make sure that they did what you had hired them to do. Suppose the company did a good job. Then you would not worry about checking on them if your sister's bicycle needed repairs a few weeks later.

Suppose the company did a bad job on your bicycle. Then you might want to replace them or watch them even more closely when your sister's bicycle needed work.

The same is true with the government. We should be sure the people we "hire" (elect) can do the job we are hiring them for. Once they get the job, we should keep an eye on them to make sure they are doing that job. If they do a good job, we may not watch them as closely. If they do a bad job, we may watch them very closely and may even decide to replace them.

Participation in government is in our own self-interest. The amount of time we spend participating will probably depend on how well we think our elected officials are doing. If everything is going well, we will spend less time than if we are concerned that someone is violating our rights. If we are pleased with the government, we may vote and do little else. If we are dissatisfied, however, we will probably take other types of action.

Reviewing and using the lesson

1. How is citizen participation related to the purposes of our government? Explain why participating in government is in our own self-interest.

2. List three ways of participating in government. For each, tell why it would be an effective way of protecting your basic rights.

3. Suppose you do not choose to vote or participate in any way in government. Should you still be required to obey its laws? Why or why not?

4. If you do not think the government is protecting your basic rights, should you still be required to obey its laws? Explain your answer.

5. Does a good citizen have a responsibility to work to improve his or her society? Why or why not?

6. Should a good citizen be concerned with improving the lives of those less fortunate? Why or why not?

What decisions will you make as a citizen?

Purpose of Lesson

In the last lesson you dealt with the question of participation in government. This lesson will help you answer three related questions. First, you will examine the question, "What are my responsibilities as a citizen?" This will include a discussion of the relationship between our rights and responsibilities.

Second, you will discuss the complicated question, "What should a citizen do when he or she thinks a particular law is unjust?" Finally, you will consider the question, "Does a citizen have a responsibility to work for the common welfare?"

The lesson will give you some possible answers to these important questions. The final answers are yours to make.

What responsibilities accompany our basic rights?

Citizens of the United States do not always agree about the responsibilities of citizens. Yet, few rights can exist in a society unless the people fulfill the responsibilities that go with them. Some of the responsibilities that Americans have agreed upon over the years are listed below.

1. If you choose to live among others in a society and enjoy that society's benefits, you are responsible for obeying the society's rules.

2. If you deny others their rights, you may have to give up your own. For example, if you endanger the lives of others by driving recklessly, you may lose your right to drive.

3. If you attend a meeting and exercise your right to speak freely, you should respect other people's right to do the same. If you disrupt the meeting and deny others the right to speak, it is reasonable and fair to exclude you and deny you the right to speak there.

When laws or governmental actions conflict with a citizen's views of what is right and wrong, the citizen faces a difficult decision. The next section will help you think about that decision.

Must you obey a law you think is unjust?

In our system of government, you have a right to try to have laws changed. Until you get them changed, you are held responsible for obeying the laws.

Suppose a law requires you to do something you believe is wrong. Must you obey the law? Some people argue that since no government is perfect, a citizen's responsibility to obey the law has limits. In their view, if a law is bad, the citizen has no responsibility to obey it.

Deciding to disobey a law is a serious step. Disobeying the law has consequences, which the citizen must be prepared to accept. Throughout history, many citizens have accepted those consequences. For example, in the 1800s, the famous American philosopher Henry David Thoreau chose to go to jail rather than pay a tax to support slavery and the Mexican-American War. In the 1950s and 1960s, Dr. Martin Luther King, Jr., and others chose to go to jail to protest racial segregation laws. During the Vietnam War, many young men burned their draft cards and refused to serve in the armed forces.

Problem solving

Your class may be divided into small groups to complete the following exercise. Using a step-by-step procedure can help you reach a good decision. Read the story that follows. Then work through the steps as Mark might have done in reaching his decision. Finally, decide what you think Mark should do and explain and defend your answer before the class.

What decision would you reach?

Mark was worried. Five of his friends were going to take part in an after-school protest the next day. They were planning to demonstrate against the new school policy prohibiting the wearing of T-shirts with certain slogans. Like his friends, Mark believed that this situation was unfair to the students. He believed the T-shirts were legal and not vulgar or offensive. He felt strongly that this policy should be changed.

Mark was worried about what would happen if he joined the picket line. He might be suspended from school. This could affect his chances of being accepted by a college. He was also afraid that he might be arrested, especially if the demonstration got out of hand. An arrest on his record could keep him from getting a good job.

What are the costs and benefits of exercising your right to participate in a demonstration?

On the other hand, he did not want to let his friends down. He wanted to show his views and help change what he thought was an unjust situation as much as they did. What should Mark do? What were his alternatives?

1. Identify the problem to be solved or decision to be reached.

2. List alternative plans of action.

3. List the advantages and disadvantages of each alternative.

4. Decide what you think should be done, considering the advantages and disadvantages of the alternatives.

5. Be prepared to explain the reasons for your decision.

6. Explain how your decision reflects the basic principles of our government.

After each group has presented its decision, you may wish to complete this exercise in the following way.

1. Discuss the plans presented by the groups and vote to adopt the plan the majority favors.

2. Discuss how the procedure above could be used in other situations in which citizens have to make difficult decisions.

What is the common welfare?

The Framers believed that the people must have civic virtue if the new Constitution was to succeed. People with civic virtue put the common welfare—the good of all the people—over their own interests. Therefore, citizens should elect people to public office who will put the common welfare over narrow and local interests.

While the common welfare is clear in some cases, at other times it is hard to agree upon what it is. For example, everyone would agree that the common welfare is helped by laws against murder. But people cannot agree whether placing a high tax on goods from other countries would serve the common welfare. Some leaders say it would. Others say it would only serve the interests of particular groups in society. Such a tax on cars, for example, might be good for people who work in the automobile industry. It might not be so good for the person buying a new car.

Problem solving

Read the following situation and answer the questions that follow. Be prepared to discuss and defend your answers.

Conflicting responsibilities of a representative

Congressman Jones represents a district where many people work in factories that make shoes. These factories are laying off more and more workers because American shoes can no longer compete with those made in other countries. Shoes can be made at lower cost in other countries because the workers there are paid lower wages. These shoes are sold at lower prices than those made in America.

The low prices may be good for people buying shoes. They are not so good for the people losing their jobs because of them. The problem for Congressman Jones is this: should he support a bill that places a tax on shoes made in other countries?

- If the bill passes, more American shoes will be sold. Then, many Americans' jobs will be saved.

- If the bill passes, it will cause the price of shoes to go up. This will make them more expensive for people who need to buy them.

1. What should Congressman Jones think about in making his decision?

2. Make an argument in favor of his supporting the tax.

3. Now make an argument against his supporting the tax.

4. What would you do if you were the Congressman? Why?

What should Congressman Jones consider when making his decision?

What are your responsibilities as a citizen?

You have learned a great deal about our nation's government. You have learned about the government's responsibilities and your rights. You have also examined some of the responsibilities of citizens, including your own. You will face many difficult decisions as a citizen.

Citizens have good reasons to develop informed opinions about their rights and responsibilities. If citizens do not understand these things, their rights are not safe and the advantages of constitutional democracy are in danger.

Reviewing and using the lesson

1. There are many ways to define the common welfare. Some say it is the greatest happiness of the greatest number of people. Others say it is the benefits shared by all members of the community. How would you define the common welfare? Explain why you think your definition is best. Give examples of how it could be used in making decisions about actual political problems, such as keeping the streets safe or the air and water clean.

2. Write a short essay in which you describe the qualities of good citizens in a constitutional democracy. Explain why you think these qualities are necessary.

3. Discuss the following questions in groups of two or three students. Each student should write his or her answers to the questions.

   - What should a person do when a law is bad? Explain your answer and give examples.

   - Suppose you cannot agree upon what is in the common interest. Should you pursue your own interests or still try to consider the interests of others? Explain your answer and provide examples.

REFERENCE SECTION

Glossary

abridge. Take away; reduce; diminish.

absolute power. Power without limits.

alien. A foreign-born resident of this country.

amendment. A change in or an addition to a document.

Anti-Federalists. The Founders who were against ratifying the Constitution because they thought it gave too much power to the national government and did not protect the rights of the people.

appellate court. A judicial body that hears appeals from a lower court.

appellate jurisdiction. The legal authority of a court to hear appeals from a lower court.

aristocrats. The wealthy, upper class who are often part of the ruling class in a government.

Articles of Confederation. The constitution of the thirteen original American states, adopted in 1781 and replaced in 1788 by the U.S. Constitution.

autocratic or dictatorial government. A government in which the rulers, whether one or many, exercise unlimited power.

basic rights. The fundamental rights to life, liberty, and property.

Bill of Rights. The first ten amendments to the Constitution which restrict the federal government's power to take away certain basic rights of the people.

Brown v. Board of Education (1954). A Supreme Court case which held that racially segregated schools were unconstitutional because they denied black children the equal protection of the laws under the 14th Amendment.

censor. To examine in order to delete anything considered objectionable.

cabinet. The heads of the departments of the executive branch, who advise the president.

checks and balances. The sharing and balancing of power among the different branches of government so no one branch can dominate the others.

citizen. A member of a state who owes allegiance to the government and is entitled to its protection.

civic virtue. The dedication of citizens to the common welfare above their own individual interests.

colonial governments. The governments set up in each of the thirteen British colonies in what is now the United States.

common people. Those who were free men (not serfs) and not members of the nobility. In Great Britain, the common people are represented in the House of Commons.

common welfare. The good of the community as a whole.

compromise. A way to settle differences by each side agreeing to give up some of what it wants.

confederation. A form of political organization in which states combine for certain purposes, such as defense, but retain their individual sovereignty. The United States was a confederation from 1776 to 1788.

Connecticut Compromise. see Great Compromise.

constitution. A set of customs, traditions, rules, and laws that describe the way a government is organized and operated.

constitutional government. A government in which the powers of the ruler or rulers are limited by a constitution, which they must obey.

Declaration of Independence. A document, written by Thomas Jefferson in 1776, in which the thirteen colonies stated their reasons for freeing themselves from British rule.

delegate. A person chosen to act for or represent others, as at a convention.

dissenting opinion. An opinion of a justice that is in disagreement with the court's decision in a case.

due process clause. As interpreted by the courts, this clause in the Fifth and Fourteenth Amendments requires that a person be treated fairly by the government.

electoral college. The electors chosen by each state who cast the official votes for president after a presidential election.

English Bill of Rights. An act passed by Parliament in 1689 which limited the power of the monarch. It established Parliament as the most powerful branch of the English government.

enumerated powers. Powers that are specifically granted to Congress in Article I, Section 8 of the Constitution.

equal protection clause. The clause in the Fourteenth Amendment that prohibits states from discriminating against people by denying them the "equal protection of the laws."

equal representation. The system by which all states would have the same number of representatives in Congress, regardless of population. The Senate is based on equal representation.

establishment clause. The clause in the First Amendment that says the government may not set up, or establish, an official religion.

executive branch. The branch of government that carries out the laws made by the legislative branch.

factions. Groups, according to James Madison, that seek to promote their own special interests at the expense of the common welfare.

federal system (or federalism). A form of government in which power is divided between a central government and subdivisions such as state and local governments.

Federalist, The. A series of articles, written in 1787-1788 by Alexander Hamilton, James Madison, and John Jay, supporting the ratification of the Constitution.

Federalist Party. Led by Alexander Hamilton, this was one of the first political parties in America. The Federalist party supported a strong national government. It believed in a broad interpretation of the powers of the national government under the Constitution.

Federalists. (1) The people who supported the ratification of the Constitution and argued for a strong central government. (2) The members of the Federalist Party.

feudalism. A system of government in which the monarch shared power with the nobility who received services from the common people.

Founders. The people who played important roles in the development of the new nation, the United States.

Framers. The delegates to the Philadelphia Convention of 1787.

free exercise clause. The part of the First Amendment that says the government shall make no law denying an individual the right to practice his religious beliefs.

freedom of expression. The freedoms of speech, press, assembly, and petition that are protected by the First Amendment.

fugitive slave clause. That part of Article IV of the Constitution which said that slaves who escaped to other states must be returned to their owners.

Glorious Revolution (1688). The struggle that overthrew King James II and established Parliament's supremacy in the English government.

government. The organization through which political authority is exercised in a society.

governor. The head of the executive branch of a state government who carries out and enforces the law.

grandfather clause. The law, in many southern states, that allowed whites who could not pass a literacy test to vote if their grandfathers had been eligible to vote.

Great Compromise (Connecticut Compromise). The plan accepted at the Philadelphia Convention that called for Congress to be composed of a Senate based on equal representation for each state and a House of Representatives based on population.

higher law. In legal systems, a set of laws such as a constitution, superior to other laws. In natural rights philosophy, the natural or God-given law which is superior to all laws made by people.

impeach. To charge a public official with a crime committed while he or she is in office.

incorporation. The process by which the Supreme Court interpreted the 14th Amendment to extend the protections of the Bill of Rights to actions by the states.

indentured servant. A person who agreed to work for another for a set period of time in return for passage to America.

Jim Crow laws. Those laws common in the South after the 1880s which required blacks to use separate schools and other public facilities.

judicial branch. The branch of government that interprets and applies the laws and settles disputes through a system of courts.

judicial review. The power of the courts to declare laws and actions of the local, state, or national government invalid if they violate the Constitution.

Judiciary Act of 1789. The law that established the federal court system below the Supreme Court.

jurisdiction. The power to interpret and apply the law; the territory within which that authority may be exercised.

legislative branch. The branch of government that makes the laws.

literacy test. A test given to people to prove they were able to read and write as a qualification for voting. In the South, these tests were used to keep blacks from voting.

literate. Able to read and write.

loyalists. Americans who supported Great Britain in the Revolutionary War.

magistrates. Judges in the colonial governments in America.

Magna Carta. A contract between King John and his nobles signed in 1215. The agreement established that the king must obey the law and it protected certain rights of the people.

Marbury v. Madison (1803). A case in which the Supreme Court held that it had the power of judicial review over acts of Congress and the President.

monarchy. A form of government in which political power is held by a single hereditary ruler such as a king or queen.

national government. The organization exercising political power in an entire nation or country, as distinguished from state and local governments.

natural rights. The rights to life, liberty, and property which all people have because they are human beings.

naturalization. The process by which an alien becomes a citizen.

necessary and proper clause. The clause (Article I, Section 8) that gives Congress the right to make all laws "necessary and proper" to carry out the powers given it in the Constitution; also called the "elastic clause."

New Jersey Plan. This plan, presented to the Philadelphia Convention, called for a one-house national legislature with each state having equal representation.

nobility. The English upper class, consisting of the titled aristocracy, represented by the House of Lords in Parliament.

Northwest Ordinance of 1787. One of the great accomplishments of the government under the Articles of Confederation. This law provided for the settlement of the western lands and for their admission into the Union.

null and void. Of no legal force; invalid.

opinion. A formal expression by a court of its reasons for a legal decision.

original jurisdiction. The legal authority of a court to be the first to hear a case.

parochial school. A private school run by a religious organization.

Parliament. The British legislature, made up of two houses, the House of Lords and the House of Commons.

petition. A document making a formal written request, usually accompanied by the signatures of a number of citizens.

Philadelphia Convention. The meeting held in Philadelphia in 1787 at which the U.S. Constitution was written.

philosopher. Someone who studies and contributes to the understanding of fundamental ideas.

politics. The activities of (1) getting and holding public office and (2) forming government policy, including laws.

poll tax. A tax that voters in many southern states were required to pay before they could vote. It was used to prevent blacks from voting.

political parties. Groups organized to promote particular political views and support candidates for public office who share those views.

popular sovereignty. The idea that the people have the ultimate power and that government is based upon the consent of the people.

private domain. Areas of a person's life that are not subject to governmental control.

proportional representation. The system under which the number of representatives a state has in the House of Representatives is based on its population.

protective tariffs. Taxes on imported goods intended to protect the industry of the home country.

ratification. The formal approval of the Constitution by the states.

ratifying conventions. Meetings held in the states to approve the Constitution.

register. To enroll one's name officially as a requirement for voting.

representative government. A system of government in which power is held by the people and exercised by elected representatives.

republic. A form of government in which the supreme political power resides with the people. The government is administered by officers elected by the people to serve their interests.

Republican Party. An early political party, led by Thomas Jefferson, that wanted to limit the powers of the national government.

royalty. The king or other royal persons. It can also mean that part of the government that represents the monarch.

segregation. The separation or isolation of a race, class, or ethnic group from the rest of society.

self-sufficient. Able to provide all the necessities of life for oneself.

separate but equal. The argument, once upheld by the Supreme Court, that separate public facilities for blacks and whites were constitutional if the facilities were of equal quality.

separation of powers. The division of powers among the different branches of government; in the United States, among the legislative, executive, and judicial branches.

Shays' Rebellion. An uprising by Massachusetts farmers in 1786 that convinced many people the Articles of Confederation needed to be changed.

slavery. Involuntary servitude; owning people as property.

social contract. The agreement among all the people in a society to give up part of their freedom to a government in return for the protection of their natural rights by that government.

sovereignty. The ultimate power in a state; in the United States, sovereignty rests with the people.

state of nature. An imaginary situation of people living in a society without government and laws.

subject. A person who is ruled by the sovereign of a nation.

suffrage. The right to vote.

supremacy clause. The clause of the Constitution (Article VI, Section 2) that states that the Constitution, the laws passed by Congress, and the treaties of the United States are the nation's highest laws and must be obeyed by the states.

three-fifths clause. A clause in the Constitution, no longer in effect, that provided for counting each slave as three-fifths of a person for purposes of representation and taxation.

unitary government. A system of government in which states or local governments exercise only those powers given them by the national government.

veto. The constitutional power of the President to refuse to sign a bill passed by Congress.

Virginia Plan. This plan, presented to the Philadelphia Convention, provided for a national government composed of three branches. It also provided for a Congress with two houses, both of which would be based on proportional representation.

Biographies of the Framers

Baldwin, Abraham (1754-1807). Baldwin was born in Connecticut. He attended Yale, where he studied the classics and law. He moved to Georgia in 1784. He served Georgia as a state legislator, in the Continental Congress, at the Philadelphia Convention, in the House of Representatives, and in the U.S. Senate. He also founded the University of Georgia. As a national legislator, Baldwin supported states' rights, though he had argued for a strong national government at the Philadelphia Convention.

Bassett, Richard (1745-1815). Bassett was born in Maryland. He studied law in Philadelphia and set up his law practice in Delaware. He was also a planter, owning three homes in Delaware and Maryland. Bassett served in the Continental Army during the Revolutionary War and participated in Delaware's constitutional convention and state legislature. At the Philadelphia Convention, Bassett made no speeches. Bassett later served as a U.S. Senator, a judge, and governor of Delaware.

Bedford, Gunning (1747-1812). Like many of the Framers, Bedford was born into a large family. A roommate of James Madison at the College of New Jersey, Bedford later studied law in Philadelphia. Bedford moved to Delaware, where he practiced law and served the state as a legislator, representative to the Continental Congress, and attorney general. Bedford was a member of the committee that drafted the Great Compromise, representing the small states' point of view. After the convention, Bedford spent many years as a federal district judge.

Blair, John (1732-1800). Blair was born into a prominent Virginia family. He graduated from the College of William and Mary and studied law in London. Blair was active in the movement to gain independence from Great Britain. He was active in Virginia state government after independence was declared. At Philadelphia, Blair never spoke, usually going along with the Virginia delegation. He later served on the Supreme Court.

Blount, William (1749-1800). Blount was the eldest son of a well-established North Carolina family. He served in the Continental Army, the North Carolina state government, and the Continental Congress. Blount missed more than a month of the Philadelphia Convention and did not say much while he was there. In 1790, he moved, settling in what is now Tennessee, and was one of its first U.S. senators.

Brearly, David (1745-1790). Brearly was born and raised in New Jersey. Although he dropped out of college, he practiced law in New Jersey. He was an avid patriot. Arrested by the British for treason, Brearly was freed by a group of patriots. Brearly fought in the Revolutionary War. From 1779 to 1789, he served as the chief justice of the New Jersey supreme court. Brearly argued for the interests of the small states at the Philadelphia Convention. He served as the president of the New Jersey ratifying convention. Appointed a federal district judge in 1789, Brearly died the next year at age 45.

Broom, Jacob (1752-1810). Broom was born in Delaware. His career was varied, including farming, surveying and map-making, shipping, importing, real estate, and city government. Broom attended every session of the Philadelphia Convention.

Butler, Pierce (1744-1822). Butler was born in Ireland, the son of a member of the House of Lords. He served in the British Army until 1771, when he resigned after marrying a colonial girl. He served with the South Carolina militia in the Revolutionary War, during which he lost much of his property. Butler spoke often at the Philadelphia Convention, arguing for a strong national government and for the interests of southern slaveholders. Although he later served in the U.S. Senate, he devoted most of his time to his plantation.

Carroll, Daniel (1730-1796). Carroll was one of only two Roman Catholics to sign the Constitution. He was a member of a prominent Maryland family. He studied in Europe, returning to the United States to live the life of a planter. In 1781, Carroll was elected to the Continental Congress. He also served in the Maryland senate. Carroll arrived late at the Philadelphia Convention but attended regularly once he got there. He participated in the debates and campaigned for ratification in Maryland. Carroll served in the House of Representatives and as one of the first commissioners of the District of Columbia.

Clymer, George (1739-1813). Clymer inherited his uncle's business, which suffered as a result of British restrictions on colonial trade. He was, nevertheless, a patriot who worked hard for independence. Clymer served in the Pennsylvania legislature and the Continental Congress. Although he did not speak too often at the Philadelphia Convention, his speeches were well planned and effective. Clymer was elected to the first Congress and later served as a member of the commission that negotiated a treaty with Native Americans in Georgia.

Davie, William R. (1756-1820). Davie was born in England, moving to South Carolina in 1763. He attended college in North Carolina and New Jersey, graduating with honors. He studied law in North Carolina and practiced there until 1787. During the 1780s, he also served in the military, a career he enjoyed. Davie favored the Great Compromise, the indirect election of senators and the president, and representation for slave property. Davie did not sign the Constitution but did work for ratification. After the convention, he served as governor of North Carolina, as a state legislator, and as a peace commissioner to France, among other offices. Davie was one of the founders of the University of North Carolina.

Dayton, Jonathan (1760-1824). Dayton, a native of New Jersey, was the youngest man to sign the Constitution. As soon as he graduated from the College of New Jersey, he entered the Continental Army. After the war, Dayton studied law and set up his practice. He also served in the New Jersey legislature. Dayton was chosen to attend the Philadelphia Convention because his father and another associate decided not to. He participated in the debates and signed the Constitution, even though there were some parts of it he did not like. Dayton later served in the House of Representatives and Senate.

Dickinson, John (1732-1808). Dickinson was born in Maryland, the son of a wealthy farm family. He was educated by private tutors, then studied law in Philadelphia and London. He set up his first law practice in Philadelphia, where he served in the Pennsylvania legislature. Dickinson became famous throughout the colonies for opposing British taxation. However, he voted against independence in 1776 and did not sign the Declaration. He did enlist in the Continental Army. He headed the committee that drafted the Articles of Confederation but by 1786 believed they needed to be changed. Dickinson had the reputation of a scholar and was highly respected. He made important contributions to the Philadelphia Convention but left early due to illness. He spent his later years writing about politics.

Ellsworth, Oliver (1745-1807). Ellsworth was a member of a well-to-do Connecticut family. He graduated from the College of New Jersey, taught school, and served as a minister before going into law. He was soon considered one of Connecticut's best lawyers. Ellsworth served in the Continental Congress and was a delegate to the Philadelphia Convention. He played an important role at the convention and was one of the authors of the Great Compromise. Elected to the U.S. Senate, he was responsible for the Judiciary Act of 1789. In 1796 Ellsworth was appointed Chief Justice of the Supreme Court.

Few, William (1748-1828). Few was born in Maryland but moved to North Carolina when he was ten. In 1771, William, his father, and a brother were involved with a group of frontiersmen who opposed the Royal Governor of North Carolina. As a result, his brother was hanged and the family had to flee to Georgia. Few served in the Georgia state legislature and the Continental Congress. He missed much of the Philadelphia Convention because he was in Congress. Few became one of Georgia's first U.S. senators. In 1799, he moved to New York, where he was active in New York state politics and banking.

Fitzsimons, Thomas (1741-1811). Fitzsimons was born in Ireland, moving to America about 1760. He lived in Philadelphia, where he was a prominent businessman. He fought in the Revolutionary War, donating money to the patriots' cause. Fitzsimons served in the Continental Congress and as a Pennsylvania state legislator. He did not say much at the Philadelphia Convention, although he attended regularly and favored a strong national government. Fitzsimons served three terms in the House of Representatives but spent most of the rest of his life attending to his business interests.

Franklin, Benjamin (1706-1790). Franklin was the oldest delegate to the Philadelphia Convention. With the possible exception of George Washington, Franklin was the best-known man in America. Born into a poor family, Franklin became an inventor, scientist, diplomat, and publisher. His *Poor Richard's Almanac* was read nationwide. His career in public service was a long and varied one, including service as an ambassador to England and France and as governor of Pennsylvania. At the Philadelphia Convention, Franklin was a compromiser, using wit to bring delegates together. He played an important role in creating the Great Compromise. He favored a strong national government and argued that the Framers should trust the judgment of the people. Although he was in poor health in 1787, he missed few sessions, being carried to and from the meeting place in a special chair. Although he did not agree with everything in the Constitution, he believed that no other convention could come up with a better document.

Gerry, Elbridge (1744-1814). Gerry was born to a wealthy merchant family in Massachusetts. He attended Harvard, learning politics from Samuel Adams. Gerry was active in protests against British policies and was one of the signers of the Declaration of Independence. He often changed his mind about political issues. For example, after Shays' Rebellion, he spoke against giving the common people too much power, but he still argued for yearly elections and against giving the Senate, which was not accountable to the people, too much power. Gerry refused to sign the Constitution and worked against ratification. Throughout his life, he served in a variety of offices including that of Vice President.

Gilman, Nicholas (1755-1814). Gilman was born into a large and distinguished New Hampshire family. He served in the Continental Army, returning home after the war to work in his father's store and take part in state politics. He served in the Continental Congress, although he had a poor attendance record. Gilman arrived late at the Philadelphia Convention and made no speeches. He was important in getting New Hampshire to ratify the Constitution. He served in the House of Representatives as a Federalist and later won election to the Senate as a Republican.

Gorham, Nathaniel (1738-1796). Gorham was born in Massachusetts. He received little formal education, becoming an apprentice to a merchant at age 15. He was active in state politics and supported the revolutionary cause. He served in the Continental Congress and was an important member of the Philadelphia Convention, speaking often and serving on various committees. He worked to gain approval of the Constitution in Massachusetts. Gorham is one of the few delegates to the convention who did not serve in the new government.

Hamilton, Alexander (1755-1804). Alexander Hamilton was one of the most brilliant thinkers at the Philadelphia Convention. His origins were modest, having been born to unmarried parents in the British West Indies. As a young man, he traveled to New York City with the help of people who recognized his intelligence. He attended college until the Revolution, in which he was very active, interrupted his studies. After the war, he studied law and entered practice. He served in the Continental Congress and was one of the leaders in calling for a constitutional convention. As a delegate to the Philadelphia Convention, he played a rather small role, partly because he had to miss many sessions due to legal business, partly because he wanted a much stronger national government than did most delegates, and partly because he did not get along with the other delegates from New York. He was one of the authors of *The Federalist* and worked hard for ratification in New York. He served in Washington's government as Secretary of the Treasury and was a leader of the Federalist

Party. In 1804, Hamilton was killed in a duel with Aaron Burr.

Houston, William (1757-?). Not a great deal is known about William Houston of Georgia. He was a member of the Continental Congress and represented Georgia in a boundary dispute with South Carolina in 1785. One of his fellow delegates to the Philadelphia Convention described him as a "gentleman of family" with little or no legal or political knowledge. He did not sign the Constitution.

Houston, William C. (1746-1788). William C. Houston studied at the College of New Jersey, where he later taught. He served in the military during the Revolutionary War and represented New Jersey in the Continental Congress. He also served as a collector of continental taxes in New Jersey, not a rewarding job during the time the Articles of Confederation were in effect. Houston did not sign the Constitution.

Ingersoll, Jared (1749-1822). Ingersoll was born in Connecticut, the son of a British colonial official. He graduated from Yale and then managed his father's business affairs. He followed his father to Philadelphia, where he studied law. Ingersoll attended every session of the Philadelphia Convention, although he said little. His service after the convention was extensive, holding such jobs as attorney general of Pennsylvania and presiding judge of the Philadelphia District Court. He once ran for Vice President, but lost. In his successful law practice, he argued several important cases before the Supreme Court.

Jenifer, Daniel of St. Thomas (1723-1790). Jenifer was born in Maryland. Not much is known about his early years. As an adult, he owned a large estate near Annapolis. He supported the Revolution, serving in the Continental Congress and the Maryland state legislature. Jenifer favored a stronger national government. Although he did not speak often at the Philadelphia Convention, he generally supported the positions of James Madison.

Johnson, William Samuel (1727-1819). Johnson was born in Connecticut. He graduated from Yale and became a lawyer. He held a number of positions in his home state prior to the Revolution, in which he found it difficult to choose sides. He finally decided that his role should be one of peacemaker, which was what he attempted to do during the war. After the war, he was a powerful member of the Continental Congress. He played an important role in the Philadelphia Convention, serving as the chairman of the committee of style, which drafted the final document. He worked for ratification in Connecticut, which he later represented in the Senate. He retired from political office to devote his time to his position as president of Columbia College.

King, Rufus (1755-1827). King was born in what is now Maine. He was the eldest son of a wealthy farmer-merchant and graduated from Harvard. He studied the law and entered practice in Massachusetts. An excellent speaker and early opponent of slavery, King served in the Massachusetts legislature and the Continental Congress. One of the youngest delegates to the Philadelphia Convention, King was also one of the best speakers, arguing for a stronger national government. His notes on the events at the convention have been of interest to historians. In 1788, King moved to New York, where he became active in state politics and was chosen as a U.S. senator several times. He also served as a director of the First Bank of the United States and as Minister to Great Britain. He ran for Vice President twice and President once, but lost all three times.

Langdon, John (1741-1819). Langdon was a native of New Hampshire. He did not receive a great deal of education and began as an apprentice to a merchant. He invested his money in trade and became a wealthy man. Langdon avidly supported the Revolution, leading colonists in a raid on British gunpowder stores, serving in public office, and pledging money to finance various military campaigns. Langdon paid his own way and that of the other New Hampshire delegate to the Philadelphia Convention. He played an important role at the convention, even though he arrived late. He favored a more powerful national government and worked for ratification in New Hampshire. His later service included duty as governor of his home state and U.S. senator.

Lansing, John (1754-1829). Lansing was born in Albany, New York, to a family that had been in America since the 1600s. He practiced law in New York and served in the state legislature and the Continental Congress. He left the Philadelphia Convention in July, along with another New York delegate, because he opposed the creation of an entirely new government. He believed that the Articles of Confederation should only have been amended. He worked against ratification of the Constitution in New York. Lansing devoted the years after the convention to various public offices in the state of New York.

Livingston, William (1723-1790). Livingston was raised by his grandmother in Albany, New York. He spent one of his teenage years as a missionary among the Mohawk Indians. He graduated from Yale and spent many years in law practice and politics in New York. Tired of law and having lost

power in the New York legislature, he moved to New Jersey around 1770. He planned to live in retirement, but instead was caught up in the Revolution. Livingston served in the Continental Congress, in the New Jersey militia, and as governor of the state. At the Philadelphia Convention, he served as chairman of the committee that reached a compromise on slavery (an institution he opposed). He worked for ratification in New Jersey, where his position as governor helped. He served as governor from 1776 until his death.

Madison, James (1751-1836). The "Father of the Constitution" was born to a wealthy Virginia family. He was taught at home and in private schools, then graduated from the College of New Jersey. While debating whether to become a lawyer or minister, Madison became involved in the revolutionary cause, thereby entering state and local politics. His poor health kept him from serving in the military. In 1780, Madison was chosen to serve in the Continental Congress, where he played a major role. He was one of the most influential voices calling for a constitutional convention. He came to the Philadelphia Convention with a plan for the new government, took extensive notes on the proceedings, spoke more than 150 times, and worked tirelessly on various committees. As one of the authors of *The Federalist*, Madison was also a key figure in the battle for ratification. Following the convention, Madison served as a member of the U.S. House of Representatives, helping to frame the Bill of Rights and organize the executive department. Under Jefferson, Madison served as Secretary of State. He then succeeded Jefferson as President. In retirement, Madison continued to speak out on public issues.

Martin, Alexander (1740-1807). Martin was born in New Jersey around 1740. He moved to North Carolina after graduating from the College of New Jersey. He served in various local and state offices and was in the military for two years. Martin returned to North Carolina and various state offices. He attended the Philadelphia Convention, but left early and did not sign the document. After the convention, he served as governor, as a U.S. senator, and as a state senator.

Martin, Luther (1748-1826). Luther Martin was born in New Jersey around 1748. After graduating from the College of New Jersey, he moved to Maryland where he practiced law. He served as state attorney general and in the Continental Congress. At the Philadelphia Convention, he opposed increasing the power of the federal government. Martin believed in the rights of the states and of the people and wanted each state to have an equal vote in Congress. He also wanted a bill of rights. Although he owned six slaves, Martin opposed slavery, speaking out against it. Because he lost the battles on the issues he thought were important, Martin left the convention and did not sign the Constitution. He fought against ratification in Maryland. After 27 years in office, Martin resigned as Maryland attorney general in 1805. He served in several other positions, but returned as attorney general in 1818.

Mason, George (1725-1792). George Mason was born into a wealthy Virginia family. He studied law and managed his large plantation near George Washington's home. Throughout most of his life, Mason preferred private life to public service, although he did serve in the Virginia legislature. At the Philadelphia Convention, Mason spoke often. He argued against giving the president too much power, for a bill of rights, and against slavery (although at his death, he owned 300 slaves). Mason did not sign the Constitution and fought against its ratification. He died shortly after the ratification of the Bill of Rights.

McClurg, James (1746-1823). McClurg was born in Virginia, the state he later represented at the Philadelphia Convention. He traveled to Scotland to study medicine. After receiving his degree in 1770, he studied in Paris and London. In 1773, he returned to Virginia, where he served as physician general and director of hospitals during the Revolution. He was named a delegate to the Philadelphia Convention when Patrick Henry and Richard Henry Lee refused to attend. He did not sign the Constitution, which he had hoped would include a life term for the president and a federal veto on state laws. His involvement in politics after the convention was minimal as he chose to devote his time to medicine.

McHenry, James (1723-1816). McHenry was another delegate born in Ireland. He came to America alone in 1771; the next year, he talked his family into coming too. He studied poetry and medicine and did hospital work during the Revolution. In 1781 he left the military to join the Maryland Senate. He also served in the Continental Congress. He was called away from the Philadelphia Convention because of family illness and missed all of June and July's sessions. After the convention, he served in the Maryland legislature and as Secretary of War. After retiring in 1800, he spent much of his time writing.

Mercer, John Francis (1750-1821). Mercer was born in Virginia and was educated at the College of William and Mary. He enlisted in the army and served from 1776 to 1779. He studied law under Thomas Jefferson and practiced in Virginia. He served in the Virginia legislature and in the Continental Congress. He moved to Maryland in 1785

when he inherited land. At the Philadelphia Convention, he opposed a strong central government and left before the convention was over. He opposed ratification. He later served in the Maryland legislature, in the U.S. House of Representatives, and as governor of Maryland.

Mifflin, Thomas (1744-1800). Thomas Mifflin was a Pennsylvania Quaker, the son of a rich merchant and politician. He was educated in Philadelphia and entered business upon finishing his education. He was also involved in politics, raising troops and serving in the Continental Army. He was expelled from the Quaker church for doing so. He served in the state legislature and in the Continental Congress. He attended the Philadelphia Convention, but did not speak. He continued in the Pennsylvania legislature and later served ten years as governor.

Morris, Gouverneur (1752-1816). Morris was born in New York to a wealthy family with a history of public service. Early in life, he lost a leg in a carriage accident. He graduated from King's College in New York City and studied law. Many of his family and friends were loyalists, but Morris sided with the patriots. He served in the militia as well as in the New York legislature and the Continental Congress. When he was defeated for Congress in 1779, Morris moved to Philadelphia to practice law. At the Philadelphia Convention, Morris gave more speeches than anyone else. He favored a strong national government ruled by the upper classes. He served on many committees and was the primary author of the actual document. After the convention, Morris spent ten years in Europe. He served briefly in the Senate, but then retired.

Morris, Robert (1734-1806). Morris was born in England. He came to America when he was 13. He was educated in Philadelphia and worked there in a shipping-banking firm. As a member of the Continental Congress, he voted against independence, but still worked hard on behalf of the new nation. He served as superintendent of finance under the Articles of Confederation, a very difficult job. At the Philadelphia Convention, Morris said little, although he was known to sympathize with those wanting a stronger central government.

Paterson, William (1745-1806). Born in Ireland, Paterson was brought to the colonies when he was two years old. The family moved often--from Delaware to Connecticut to New Jersey, where they finally settled. Paterson graduated from the College of New Jersey and studied law. He supported the patriots in the Revolutionary War. Paterson served as attorney general of New Jersey from 1776-1783. At the Philadelphia Convention, he argued strongly for the rights of the small states, putting forth the New Jersey Plan in opposition to Madison's Virginia Plan. Although he left the convention in July, he returned to sign the Constitution. Later, Paterson served as a U.S. senator, governor of New Jersey, and as a Supreme Court justice.

Pierce, William (1740-1789). It is believed that Pierce was born in Georgia, the state he represented at the Philadelphia Convention, although he often referred to himself as a Virginian. He served in the Revolutionary War, returning to Georgia in 1783 to attend to his personal business. At the Philadelphia Convention, Pierce spoke three times, leaving early. Although he did not sign the document, it is not known whether he actually opposed the Constitution. He is perhaps best known for writing notes on the convention in which he described the personalities of the other delegates.

Pinckney, Charles (1757-1824). Charles Pinckney was born in South Carolina, the son of a rich lawyer and planter. He trained as a lawyer. He served in the militia during the Revolution, was captured by the British, and remained a prisoner until 1781. He served in the Continental Congress and the South Carolina legislature. At the Philadelphia Convention, Pinckney spoke often. He was a good speaker who contributed to the compromises that made the Constitution possible. After the convention, he held a variety of political offices, including governor and U.S. senator. Although he began his career as a Federalist, he switched to the Republican party and worked to give the vote to all white males. The last public office he held was a seat in the U.S. House of Representatives.

Pinckney, Charles Cotesworth (1746-1825). The cousin of the younger Pinckney, Charles Cotesworth was also a native of South Carolina. He was educated in England, where his father was representing South Carolina. In 1769, he returned home to practice law. He served in the military during the Revolution and was held as a prisoner for two years. After the war, he practiced law and served in the South Carolina legislature. Pinckney attended every session of the Philadelphia Convention, arguing for a strong central government. He was an important delegate who contributed to compromises on troublesome issues. He worked for ratification in South Carolina. Pinckney was a Federalist, who ran for vice-president once and president twice, losing all three times. He continued to practice law and serve in the South Carolina legislature.

Randolph, Edmund (1753-1813). Randolph was born into a prominent Virginia family of lawyers. He kept the family tradition, attending the College of William and Mary and then studying law under his father. The Revolution split the family, with the father, mother, and two sisters being loyalists and Edmund and his uncle patriots. Randolph served in the Continental Congress and as governor of Virginia. He gave the first major speech at the Philadelphia Convention, in which he criticized the Articles of Confederation. As the leader of the Virginia delegation to the convention, Randolph presented the Virginia Plan, calling for a stronger national government and proportional representation in Congress. Although the Constitution eventually included many ideas similar to those in the Virginia Plan, Randolph did not sign the document. However, George Washington convinced him to support ratification. Randolph served as attorney general and secretary of state under Washington.

Read, George (1733-1798). Read was born in Maryland, but his family moved to Delaware soon after his birth. He attended schools in Pennsylvania and studied law in Philadelphia. In 1754, he set up a practice in Delaware. He supported "dignified" protests against British actions and voted against independence in 1776, but did sign the Declaration. During the Revolution, Read was busy with state activities. Poor health caused him to retire temporarily in 1779, but he returned to the service of his state in 1782. At the Philadelphia Convention, Read argued for the rights of the small states and for a strong executive. He led the ratification battle in Delaware. Read served in the U.S. Senate for four years, resigning to take the post of chief justice of Delaware, which he held until his death.

Rutledge, John (1739-1800). Rutledge was born in South Carolina and was educated at home by his father and a tutor. He then studied law in London and returned to South Carolina, where he practiced law and built a fortune. He was politically active in South Carolina in the 1760s and 1770s, being elected to the Continental Congress and to the governorship. When the British seized Charleston, Rutledge had to flee to North Carolina, where he gathered a force to recapture South Carolina. He continued to be politically active through the 1780s. At the Philadelphia Convention, he was an important delegate, speaking often and effectively. He argued strongly for the interests of southern states. Washington appointed Rutledge to the Supreme Court where he served a brief time, returning to South Carolina to serve on the state supreme court. In 1795, Washington again appointed him to the U.S. Supreme Court, this time as Chief Justice, but the Senate rejected his nomination.

Sherman, Roger (1721-1793). Born in Massachusetts, Sherman spent most of his boyhood helping his father with farming and shoe-making chores. However, he read in whatever spare time he could find. In 1743, he moved to Connecticut, purchasing a store and winning a variety of local political offices. Although Sherman had not formally studied the law, he became a lawyer. His career was distinguished, including service in the state legislature, and work as a judge. Although he gave up the practice of law in 1761, he continued his political career, serving in the Continental Congress. Sherman was one of the members of the committee that drafted the Declaration of Independence and the Articles of Confederation. He attended nearly every session of the Philadelphia Convention and was an important contributor to the Great Compromise. He also worked hard to get Connecticut to ratify the Constitution. Sherman later served as a member of the House of Representatives and the Senate.

Spaight, Richard Dobbs, Sr. (1758-1802). Spaight was born in North Carolina but was sent to Ireland after his parents died when he was eight. He was educated there and in Scotland, returning the North Carolina in 1778. He served in the state militia as well as in the state legislature. He also served in the Continental Congress after the Revolution. At the Philadelphia Convention, he attended every session and spoke on several occasions. He worked to gain ratification in North Carolina. Spaight lost elections for the Senate and for governor, but was elected to the House in 1798.

Strong, Caleb (1745-1819). Strong was born in Massachusetts. He graduated from Harvard with honors. In his early twenties, he contracted smallpox which damaged his sight. He became a lawyer, serving in various local and state offices in Massachusetts. He declined a seat in the Continental Congress. At the Philadelphia Convention, Strong took part until August, when he left because of an illness in the family. He did not sign the document. He was elected to the U.S. Senate in 1789, resigning in 1795 to return to his law practice. He served as governor of Massachusetts from 1800-1807 and again from 1812-1816.

Washington, George (1732-1799). Washington was born in Virginia. He grew up there on several plantations along the Potomac and Rappahannock Rivers. He was not particularly well educated, but did learn surveying. In 1753, he began his service to the country, which was to continue throughout his life, despite his desire to live a more private existence. Washington's efforts as commander of the Continental Army are well known. After the Treaty of Paris was signed in 1783, Washington returned to his home, Mount Vernon. Although he did not initially want to attend the Philadelphia Convention, his friends convinced him that his presence was necessary. He was elected president of the convention but spoke little. His presence and approval, however, were important. Nearly everyone as-

sumed that Washington would be the first President of the United States, which, of course, he was, serving from 1789-1797.

Williamson, Hugh (1735-1819). Williamson was born in Pennsylvania, the oldest child in a large family. Educated to be a minister, he instead went to Europe to study medicine. At the beginning of the Revolution, he was in Europe where he wrote a pamphlet that urged English support for the American cause. When he returned to America, he settled in North Carolina, where he practiced medicine, serving as surgeon-general for the state's troops. He was an active delegate to the Philadelphia Convention, serving on five committees and debating skillfully. He worked for ratification and served two terms in the U.S. House.

Wilson, James (1741-1798). Wilson was born and educated in Scotland. He arrived in America in 1765, where he taught and studied law. He set up a legal practice in Pennsylvania. He was active in the revolutionary effort, voting for independence and signing the Declaration. After the war, he defended loyalists and their sympathizers. His shift to conservatism angered many people in Pennsylvania, but by the 1780s, Wilson was again elected to the Continental Congress. He was an influential delegate to the Philadelphia Convention, where he spoke even more often than Madison. Wilson led the ratification effort in Pennsylvania. In 1789, he was appointed to the Supreme Court.

Wythe, George (1726-1806). Wythe was born on a Virginia plantation. He attended the College of William and Mary and studied law. He entered political life, serving in the Virginia legislature and as mayor of Williamsburg. He signed the Declaration of Independence and worked actively for the Revolution. In 1779, he was named the first professor of law in a U.S. college. Although he was well respected for his knowledge and high ethical standards, he did not contribute greatly to the Philadelphia Convention, leaving early because of other obligations. He did not sign the document.

Yates, Robert (1738-1801). Yates was born and educated in New York. He became a lawyer and set up practice in Albany. He served eight years as chief justice of the New York Supreme Court. Yates left the Philadelphia Convention because he believed it had exceeded its authority. A strong Anti-Federalist, he worked against ratification, writing several essays attacking the document. Yates kept notes of the convention which have been useful to historians.

Declaration of Independence

IN CONGRESS,   JULY 4, 1776.

A DECLARATION

BY THE REPRESENTATIVES OF THE

UNITED STATES OF AMERICA,

IN GENERAL CONGRESS ASSEMBLED

WHEN in the Course of human Events, it becomes necessary for one People to dissolve the Political Bands which have connected them with another, and to assume among the Powers of the Earth, the separate and equal Station to which the Laws of Nature and of Nature's God entitle them, a decent Respect to the Opinions of Mankind requires that they should declare the causes which impel them to the Separation.

We hold these Truths to be self-evident, that all Men are created equal, that they are endowed by their Creator with certain unalienable Rights, that among these are Life, Liberty, and the Pursuit of Happiness-- That to secure these Rights, Governments are instituted among Men, deriving their just Powers from the Consent of the Governed, that whenever any Form of Government becomes destructive of these Ends it is the Right of the People to alter or to abolish it, and to institute new Government, laying its Foundation on such Principles, and organizing its Powers in such Form, as to them shall seem most likely to effect their Safety and Happiness. Prudence, indeed, will dictate that Governments long established should not be changed for light and transient Causes; and accordingly all Experience hath shewn, that Mankind are more disposed to suffer, while Evils are sufferable, than to right themselves by abolishing the Forms to which they are accustomed. But when a long Train of Abuses and Usurpations, pursuing invariably the same Object, evinces a Design to reduce them under absolute Despotism, it is their Right, it is their Duty, to throw off such Government, and to provide new Guards for their future Security. Such has been the patient Sufferance of these Colonies; and such is now the Necessity which constrains them to alter their former Systems of Government. The History of the present King of Great-Britain is a History of repeated Injuries and Usurpations, all having in direct Object the Establishment of an absolute Tyranny over these States. To prove this, let Facts be submitted to a candid World.

He has refused his Assent to Laws, the most wholesome and necessary for the public Good.

He has forbidden his Governors to pass Laws of immediate and pressing Importance, unless suspended in their Operation till his Assent should be obtained; and when so suspended, he has utterly neglected to attend to them.

He has refused to pass other Laws for the Accommodation of large Districts of People, unless those People would relinquish the Right of Representation in the Legislature, a Right inestimable to them, and formidable to Tyrants only.

He has called together Legislative Bodies at Places unusual, uncomfortable, and distant from the Depository of their public Records, for the sole Purpose of fatiguing them into Compliance with his Measures.

He has dissolved Representative Houses repeatedly, for opposing with manly Firmness his Invasions on the Rights of the People.

He has refused for a long Time, after such Dissolutions, to cause others to be elected; whereby the Legislative Powers, incapable of Annihilation, have returned to the People at large for their exercise; the State remaining in the mean time exposed to all the Dangers of Invasions from without, and Convulsions within.

He has endeavored to prevent the Population of these States; for that Purpose obstructing the Laws for Naturalization of Foreigners; refusing to pass others to encourage their Migrations hither, and raising the Conditions of new Appropriations of Lands.

He has obstructed the Administration of Justice, by refusing his Assent to Laws for establishing Judiciary Powers.

He has made Judges dependent on his Will alone, for the Tenure of their Offices, and the Amount and Payment of their Salaries.

He has erected a Multitude of new Offices, and sent hither Swarms of Officers to harass our People and eat out their Substance.

He has kept among us, in Times of Peace, Standing Armies, without the consent of our Legislatures.

He has affected to render the Military independent of and superior to the Civil Power.

He has combined with others to subject us to a Jurisdiction foreign to our Constitution, and unacknowledged by our Laws; giving his Assent to their Acts of pretended Legislation:

For quartering large Bodies of Armed Troops among us:

For protecting them, by a mock Trial, from Punishment for any Murders which they should commit on the Inhabitants of these States:

For cutting off our Trade with all Parts of the World:

For imposing Taxes on us without our Consent:

For depriving us, in many Cases, of the Benefits of Trial by Jury:

For transporting us beyond Seas to be tried for pretended Offenses:

For abolishing the free System of English Laws in a neighbouring Province, establishing therein an Arbitrary Government, and enlarging its Boundaries, so as to render it at once an Example and fit Instrument for introducing the same absolute Rule into these Colonies:

For taking away our Charters, abolishing our most valuable Laws, and altering fundamentally the Forms of our Governments:

For suspending our own Legislatures, and declaring themselves invested with Power to legislate for us in all Cases whatsoever.

He has abdicated Government here, by declaring us out of his Protection and waging War against us.

He has plundered our Seas, ravaged our Coasts, burnt our Towns, and destroyed the Lives of our People.

He is, at this Time, transporting large Armies of foreign Mercenaries to compleat the Works of Death, Desolation, and Tyranny, already begun with circumstances of Cruelty and Perfidy, scarcely paralleled in the most barbarous Ages, and totally unworthy the Head of a civilized Nation.

He has constrained our fellow Citizens taken Captive on the high Seas to bear Arms against their Country, to become the Executioners of their Friends and Brethren, or to fall themselves by their Hands.

He has excited domestic Insurrections amongst us, and has endeavoured to bring on the Inhabitants of our Frontiers, the merciless Indian Savages, whose known Rule of Warfare, is an undistinguished Destruction, of all Ages, Sexes and Conditions.

In every stage of these Oppressions we have Petitioned for Redress in the most humble Terms: Our repeated Petitions have been answered only by repeated Injury. A Prince, whose Character is thus marked by every act which may define a Tyrant, is unfit to be the Ruler of a free People.

Nor have we been wanting in Attentions to our British Brethren. We have warned them from Time to Time of Attempts by their Legislature to extend an unwarrantable Jurisdiction over us. We have reminded them of the Circumstances of our Emigration and Settlement here. We have appealed to their native Justice and Magnanimity, and we have conjured them by the Ties of our common Kindred to disavow these Usurpations, which, would inevitably interrupt our Connections and Correspondence. They too have been deaf to the Voice of Justice and of Consanguinity. We must, therefore, acquiesce in the Necessity, which denounces our Separation, and hold them, as we hold the rest of Mankind, Enemies in War, in Peace, Friends.

We, therefore, the Representatives of the UNITED STATES OF AMERICA, in GENERAL CONGRESS, Assembled, appealing to the Supreme Judge of the World for the Rectitude of our Intentions, do, in the Name, and by Authority of the good People of these Colonies, solemnly Publish and Declare, That these United Colonies are, and of Right ought to be, FREE AND INDEPENDENT STATES; that they are absolved from all Allegiance to the British Crown, and that all political Connection between them and the State of Great-Britain, is and ought to be totally dissolved; and that as FREE AND INDEPENDENT STATES, they have full Power to levy War, conclude Peace, contract Alliances, establish Commerce, and to do all other Acts and Things which INDEPENDENT STATES may of right do. And for the support of this Declaration, with a firm Reliance on the Protection of divine Providence, we mutually pledge to each other our Lives, our Fortunes, and our sacred Honor.

Signed by ORDER and in BEHALF of the CONGRESS,

JOHN HANCOCK, PRESIDENT.

Signers of the Declaration of Independence

New-Hampshire
Josiah Bartlett,
Wm. Whipple,
Matthew Thornton.

Massachusetts-Bay
Saml. Adams,
John Adams,
Robt. Treat Paine,
Elbridge Gerry.

Rhode-Island and Providence, &c.
Step. Hopkins,
William Ellery.

Connecticut
Roger Sherman,
Saml. Huntington,
Wm. Williams,
Oliver Wolcott.

New-York
Wm. Floyd,
Phil. Livingston,
Frans. Lewis,
Lewis Morris.

New-Jersey
Richd. Stockton,
Jno. Witherspoon,
Fras. Hopkinson,
John Hart,
Abra. Clark.

Pennsylvania
Robt. Morris,
Benjamin Rush,
Benja. Franklin,
John Morton,
Geo. Clymer,
Jas. Smith
Geo. Taylor,
James Wilson,
Geo. Ross.

Delaware
Casar Rodney,
Geo. Read,
(Tho M:Kean.)

Maryland
Samuel Chase,
Wm. Paca,
Thos. Stone,
Charles Carroll, of Carrollton.

Virginia
George Wythe,
Richard Henry Lee,
Ths. Jefferson,
Benja. Harrison,
Thos. Nelson, jr.
Francis Lightfoot Lee,
Carter Braxton.

North-Carolina
Wm. Hooper
Joseph Hewes,
John Penn.

South-Carolina
Edward Rutledge,
Thos. Heyward, junr.
Thomas Lynch, junr.
Arthur Middleton.

Georgia
Button Gwinnett,
Lyman Hall,
Geo. Walton.

According to the authenticated list printed by order of Congress of January 18, 1777.
Spelling and abbreviations of names conform to original printed list.

The Constitution of the United States of America

Preamble

We the People of the United States, in Order to form a more perfect Union, establish Justice, insure domestic tranquility, provide for the common defence, promote the general Welfare, and secure the Blessings of Liberty to ourselves and our Posterity, do ordain and establish this Constitution for the United States of America.

ARTICLE I.

The Legislative Branch

Section 1.

All legislative Powers herein granted shall be vested in a Congress of the United States, which shall consist of a Senate and House of Representatives.

Section 2.

House of Representatives: Organization and Power of Impeachment

1. The House of Representatives shall be composed of Members chosen every second Year by the People of the several States, and the Electors in each State shall have the Qualifications requisite for Electors of the most numerous Branch of the State Legislature.

2. No Person shall be a Representative who shall not have attained to the Age of twenty five Years, and been seven Years a Citizen of the United States, and who shall not, when elected, be an Inhabitant of that State in which he shall be chosen.

3. [Representatives and direct Taxes shall be apportioned among the several States which may be included within this Union, according to their respective Numbers, which shall be determined by adding to the whole Number of free Persons, including those bound to Service for a Term of Years, and excluding Indians not taxed, three fifths of all other Persons.]* The actual Enumeration shall be made within three Years after the first Meeting of the Congress of the United States, and within every subsequent Term of ten Years, in such Manner as they shall by Law direct. The number of Representatives shall not exceed one for every thirty Thousand, but each State shall have at Least one Representative; and until such enumeration shall be made, the State of New Hampshire shall be entitled to choose three, Massachusetts eight, Rhode Island and Providence Plantations one, Connecticut five, New York six, New Jersey four, Pennsylvania eight, Delaware one, Maryland six, Virginia ten, North Carolina five, South Carolina five, and Georgia three.

4. When vacancies happen in the Representation from any State, the Executive Authority thereof shall issue Writs of Election to fill such Vacancies.

5. The House of Representatives shall choose their Speaker and other Officers; and shall have the sole Power of Impeachment.

Section 3.

The Senate, Organization and Powers of Impeachment

1. The Senate of the United States shall be composed of two Senators from each State, [chosen by the Legislature thereof,]** for six Years; and each Senator shall have one Vote.

2. Immediately after they shall be assembled in Consequence of the first Election, they shall be divided as equally as may be into three Classes. The seats of the Senators of the first Class shall be vacated at the Expiration of the second Year, of the second Class at the Expiration of the fourth Year, and of the third Class at the Expiration of the sixth Year, so that one third may be chosen every second Year; [and if Vacancies happen by Resignation, or otherwise, during the Recess of the Legislature of any State, the Executive thereof may make temporary Appointments until the next Meeting of the Legislature, which shall then fill such Vacancies.]**

3. No Person shall be a Senator who shall not have attained to the Age of thirty Years, and been nine Years a Citizen of the United States, and who shall not, when elected, be an Inhabitant of that State for which he shall be chosen.

4. The Vice President of the United States shall be President of the Senate, but shall have no Vote, unless they be equally divided.

5. The Senate shall choose their other officers, and also a President pro tempore, in the Absence of

*Changed by section 2 of the Fourteenth Amendment.

**Changed by the Seventeenth Amendment.

the Vice President, or when he shall exercise the Office of President of the United States.

6. The Senate shall have the sole Power to try all Impeachments. When sitting for that Purpose, they shall be on Oath or Affirmation. When the President of the United States is tried, the Chief Justice shall preside: And no person shall be convicted without the Concurrence of two thirds of the Members present.

7. Judgment in Cases of Impeachment shall not extend further than to removal from Office, and disqualification to hold and enjoy any Office of honor, Trust or Profit under the United States; but the Party convicted shall nevertheless be liable and subject to Indictment, Trial, Judgment and Punishment, according to Law.

Section 4.
Elections and Meeting of Congress

1. The Times, Places and Manner of holding Elections for Senators and Representatives shall be prescribed in each State by the Legislature thereof; but the Congress may at any time by Law make or alter such Regulations, except as to the Places of choosing Senators.

2. The Congress shall assemble at least once in every Year, and such Meeting shall be [on the first Monday in December,]* unless they shall by Law appoint a different Day.

Section 5.
Congress's Rules of Procedure, Powers, Quorum, Journals, Meetings, Adjournments

1. Each House shall be the Judge of the Elections, Returns and Qualifications of its own Members, and a Majority of each shall constitute a Quorum to do Business; but a smaller Number may adjourn from day to day, and may be authorized to compel the Attendance of absent Members, in such Manner, and under such Penalties as each House may provide.

2. Each House may determine the Rules of its Proceedings, punish its members for disorderly Behavior, and, with the Concurrence of two thirds, expel a Member.

3. Each House shall keep a Journal of its Proceedings, and from time to time publish the same, excepting such Parts as may in their Judgment require Secrecy; and the Yeas and Nays of the Members of either House on any question shall, at the Desire of one fifth of those Present, be entered on the Journal.

4. Neither House, during the Session of Congress, shall, without the Consent of the other, adjourn for more than three days, nor to any other Place than that in which the two Houses shall be sitting.

Section 6.
Pay, Privileges, Limitations

1. The Senators and Representatives shall receive a Compensation for their Services, to be ascertained by Law, and paid out of the Treasury of the United States. They shall in all cases, except Treason, Felony and Breach of the Peace, be privileged from Arrest during their Attendance at the Session of their respective Houses, and in going to and returning from the same; and for any Speech or Debate in either House, they shall not be questioned in any other Place.

2. No Senator or Representative shall, during the Time for which he was elected, be appointed to any civil Office under the Authority of the United States, which shall have been created, or the Emoluments whereof shall have been increased during such time; and no Person holding any Office under the United States, shall be a Member of either House during his Continuance in Office.

Section 7.
Procedure in Passing Bills, President's Veto Power

1. All Bills for raising Revenue shall originate in the House of Representatives; but the Senate may propose or concur with Amendments as on other Bills.

2. Every Bill which shall have passed the House of Representatives and the Senate, shall, before it becomes a Law, be presented to the President of the United States; if he approve he shall sign it, but if not he shall return it, with his Objections, to that House in which it shall have originated, who shall enter the Objections at large on their Journal, and proceed to reconsider it. If after such Reconsideration two thirds of that House shall agree to pass the Bill, it shall be sent, together with the Objections, to the other House, by which it shall likewise be reconsidered, and if approved by two thirds of that House, it shall become a Law. But in all such Cases the Votes of both Houses shall be determined by yeas and nays, and the Names of the Persons voting for and against the Bill shall be

*Changed by section 2 of the Twentieth Amendment.

entered on the Journal of each House respectively. If any Bill shall not be returned by the President within ten Days (Sundays excepted) after it shall have been presented to him, the Same shall be a Law, in like Manner as if he had signed it, unless the Congress by their Adjournment prevent its Return, in which Case it shall not be a Law.

3. Every Order, Resolution, or Vote to which the Concurrence of the Senate and House of Representatives may be necessary (except on a question of Adjournment) shall be presented to the President of the United States; and before the Same shall take Effect, shall be approved by him, or being disapproved by him, shall be repassed by two thirds of the Senate and House of Representatives, according to the Rules and Limitations prescribed in the Case of a Bill.

Section 8.
Powers Delegated to Congress
The Congress shall have Power

1. To lay and collect Taxes, Duties, Imposts and Excises, to pay the Debts and provide for the common Defence and general Welfare of the United States; but all Duties, Imposts and Excises shall be uniform throughout the United States;

2. To borrow Money on the credit of the United States;

3. To regulate Commerce with foreign Nations, and among the several States, and with the Indian Tribes;

4. To establish an uniform Rule of Naturalization, and uniform Laws on the subject of Bankruptcies throughout the United States;

5. To coin Money, regulate the Value thereof, and of Foreign Coin, and fix the Standard of Weights and Measures;

6. To provide for the Punishment of counterfeiting the Securities and current Coin of the United States;

7. To establish Post Offices and post Roads;

8. To promote the Progress of Science and useful Arts, by securing for limited Times to Authors and Inventors the exclusive Right to their respective Writings and Discoveries;

9. To constitute Tribunals inferior to the supreme Court;

10. To define and punish Piracies and Felonies committed on the high Seas, and Offenses against the Law of Nations;

11. To declare War, grant Letters of Marque and Reprisal, and make Rules concerning Captures on Land and Water;

12. To raise and support Armies, but no Appropriation of Money to that Use shall be for a longer Term than two Years;

13. To provide and maintain a Navy;

14. To make Rules for the Government and Regulation of the land and naval Forces;

15. To provide for calling forth the Militia to execute the Laws of the Union, suppress Insurrections and repel Invasions;

16. To provide for organizing, arming, and disciplining the Militia, and for governing such Part of them as may be employed in the Service of the United States, reserving to the States respectively, the Appointment of the Officers, and the Authority of training the Militia according to the discipline prescribed by Congress;

17. To exercise exclusive Legislation in all Cases whatsoever, over such District (not exceeding ten Miles square) as may, by Cession of particular States, and the Acceptance of Congress, become the Seat of the Government of the United States, and to exercise like Authority over all Places purchased by the Consent of the Legislature of the State in which the Same shall be, for the Erection of Forts, Magazines, Arsenals, dock-Yards and other needful Buildings;— And

18. To make all Laws which shall be necessary and proper for carrying into Execution the foregoing powers, and all other Powers vested by this Constitution in the Government of the United States, or in any Department or Officer thereof.

Section 9.
Powers Denied to Congress

1. The Migration or Importation of such Persons as any of the States now existing shall think proper to admit, shall not be prohibited by the Congress prior to the Year one thousand eight hundred and eight, but a Tax or duty may be imposed on such Importation, not exceeding ten dollars for each Person.

2. The Privilege of the Writ of Habeas Corpus shall not be suspended, unless when in Cases of

Rebellion or Invasion the public Safety may require it.

3. No Bill of Attainder or ex post facto Law shall be passed.

4. [No Capitation, or other direct, Tax shall be laid, unless in Proportion to the Census or Enumeration herein before directed to be taken.]*

5. No Tax or Duty shall be laid on Articles exported from any State.

6. No Preference shall be given by any Regulation of Commerce or Revenue to the Ports of one State over those of another: nor shall Vessels bound to, or from, one State, be obliged to enter, clear, or pay Duties in another.

7. No Money shall be drawn from the Treasury, but in Consequence of Appropriations made by Law; and a regular Statement and Account of the Receipts and Expenditures of all public Money shall be published from time to time.

8. No Title of Nobility shall be granted by the United States: And no Person holding any Office of Profit or Trust under them, shall, without the Consent of the Congress, accept of any present, Emolument, Office, or Title, of any kind whatever, from any King, Prince, or foreign State.

Section 10.

Restrictions on States' Powers

1. No State shall enter into any Treaty, Alliance, or Confederation; grant Letters of Marque and Reprisal; coin Money; emit Bills of Credit; make any Thing but gold and silver Coin a Tender in Payment of Debts; pass any Bill of Attainder, ex post facto Law, or Law impairing the Obligation of Contracts, or grant any Title of Nobility.

2. No State shall, without the Consent of the Congress, lay any Imposts or Duties on Imports or Exports, except what may be absolutely necessary for executing its inspection Laws: and the net Produce of all Duties and Imposts, laid by any State on Imports or Exports, shall be for the Use of the Treasury of the United States; and all such Laws shall be subject to the Revision and Control of the Congress.

3. No State shall, without the Consent of Congress, lay any Duty of Tonnage, keep Troops, or Ships of War in time of Peace, enter into any Agreement or Compact with another State, or with a foreign Power, or engage in War, unless actually invaded, or in such imminent Danger as will not admit of delay.

ARTICLE II.

The Executive Branch

Section 1.

President and Vice-President: Election, Qualifications, and Oath

1. The executive Power shall be vested in a President of the United States of America. He shall hold his Office during the term of four Years, and, together with the Vice President, chosen for the same Term, be elected, as follows.

2. Each State shall appoint, in such Manner as the Legislature thereof may direct, a Number of Electors, equal to the whole Number of Senators and Representatives to which the State may be entitled in the Congress: but no Senator or Representative, or Person holding an Office of Trust or Profit under the United States, shall be appointed an Elector.

3. [The Electors shall meet in their respective states, and vote by Ballot for two Persons, of whom one at least shall not be an Inhabitant of the same State with themselves. And they shall make a List of all the Persons voted for, and of the Number of Votes for each; which List they shall sign and certify, and transmit sealed to the Seat of the Government of the United States, directed to the President of the Senate. The President of the Senate shall, in the Presence of the Senate and House of Representatives, open all the Certificates, and the Votes shall then be counted. The Person having the greatest Number of Votes shall be the President, if such Number be a Majority of the whole Number of Electors appointed; and if there be more than one who have such Majority, and have an equal Number of Votes, then the House of Representatives shall immediately choose by Ballot one of them for President; and if no Person have a Majority, then from the five highest on the List the said House shall in like manner choose the President. But in choosing the President, the Votes shall be taken by States, the Representation from each State having one Vote; A quorum for this Purpose shall consist of a Member or Members from two thirds of the States, and a Majority of all the States shall be necessary to a Choice. In every Case, after the Choice of the President, the Person having the greatest Number of Votes of the Electors shall be the Vice President. But if there should remain two or more who have

*Changed by the Sixteenth Amendment.

equal Votes, the Senate shall choose from them by Ballot the Vice President.]*

4. The Congress may determine the Time of choosing the Electors, and the day on which they shall give their Votes; which Day shall be the same throughout the United States.

5. No Person except a natural born Citizen, or a Citizen of the United States at the time of the Adoption of this Constitution, shall be eligible to the Office of the President; neither shall any person be eligible to that Office who shall not have attained to the Age of thirty five Years, and been fourteen Years a Resident within the United States.

6. [In Case of the Removal of the President from Office, or of his Death, Resignation, or Inability to discharge the Powers and Duties of the said Office, the Same shall devolve on the Vice President, and the Congress may by Law provide for the Case of Removal, Death, Resignation or Inability, both of the President and Vice President, declaring what Officer shall then act as President, and such Officer shall act accordingly, until the Disability be removed, or a President shall be elected.]**

7. The President shall, at stated Times, receive for his Services, a Compensation, which shall neither be increased nor diminished during the Period for which he shall have been elected, and he shall not receive within that Period any other Emolument from the United States, or any of them.

8. Before he enter the Execution of his Office, he shall take the following Oath or Affirmation: — "I do solemnly swear (or affirm) that I will faithfully execute the Office of President of the United States, and will to the best of my Ability, preserve, protect, and defend the Constitution of the United States."

Section 2.
Powers of the President

1. The President shall be Commander in Chief of the Army and Navy of the United States, and of the Militia of the several States, when called into the actual Service of the United States; he may require the Opinion, in writing, of the principal Officer in each of the executive Departments, upon any Subject relating to the Duties of their respective Offices, and he shall have Power to grant Reprieves and Pardons for Offenses against the United States, except in Cases of Impeachment.

2. He shall have Power, by and with the Advice and Consent of the Senate, to make Treaties, provided two thirds of the Senators present concur; and he shall nominate, and by and with the Advice and Consent of the Senate, shall appoint Ambassadors, other public Ministers and Consuls, Judges of the supreme Court, and all other Officers of the United States, whose Appointments are not herein otherwise provided for, and which shall be established by Law: but the Congress may by Law vest the Appointment of such inferior Officers, as they think proper, in the President alone, in the Courts of Law, or in the Heads of Departments.

3. The President shall have Power to fill up all Vacancies that may happen during the Recess of the Senate, by granting Commissions which shall expire at the End of their next Session.

Section 3.
Duties of the President

He shall from time to time give to the Congress Information of the State of the Union, and recommend to their Consideration such Measures as he shall judge necessary and expedient; he may, on extraordinary Occasions, convene both Houses, or either of them, and in Case of Disagreement between them, with Respect to the Time of Adjournment, he may adjourn them to such Time as he shall think proper; he shall receive Ambassadors and other public Ministers; he shall take Care that the Laws be faithfully executed, and shall Commission all the Officers of the United States.

Section 4.
Impeachment and Removal from Office for Crimes

The President, Vice President and all civil Officers of the United States, shall be removed from Office on Impeachment for, and Conviction of, Treason, Bribery, or other high Crimes and Misdemeanors.

ARTICLE III.
The Judicial Branch

Section 1.
Federal Courts, Tenure of Office

The judicial Power of the United States, shall be vested in one supreme Court, and in such inferior Courts as the Congress may from time to time ordain and establish. The Judges, both of the supreme and inferior Courts, shall hold their Offices during good Behavior, and shall, at stated

*Changed by the Twelfth Amendment.
**Changed by the Twenty-Fifth Amendment.

Times, receive for their Services a Compensation, which shall not be diminished during their Continuance in Office.

Section 2.
Jurisdiction of Federal Courts

1. The judicial Power shall extend to all Cases, in Law and Equity, arising under this Constitution, the Laws of the United States, and Treaties made, or which shall be made, under their Authority;— to all Cases affecting Ambassadors, other public Ministers and Consuls;— to all Cases of admiralty and maritime Jurisdiction;— to Controversies to which the United States shall be a Party;— to Controversies between two or more States; [between a State and Citizens of another State;]* between Citizens of different States;—between Citizens of the same State claiming Lands under Grants of different States;—[and between a State, or the Citizens thereof, and foreign States, Citizens or Subjects.]*

2. In all Cases affecting Ambassadors, other public Ministers and Consuls, and those in which a State shall be Party, the supreme Court shall have original Jurisdiction. In all the other Cases before mentioned, the supreme Court shall have appellate Jurisdiction, both as to Law and Fact, with such Exceptions, and under such Regulations as the Congress shall make.

3. The Trial of all Crimes, except in Cases of Impeachment, shall be by Jury; and such Trial shall be held in the State where said Crimes shall have been committed; but when not committed within any State, the Trial shall be at such Place or Places as the Congress may by Law have directed.

Section 3.
Treason: Conviction Of and Punishment For

1. Treason against the United States shall consist only in levying War against them, or in adhering to their Enemies, giving them Aid and Comfort. No Person shall be convicted of Treason unless on the Testimony of two Witnesses to the same overt Act, or on Confession in open Court.

2. The Congress shall have Power to declare the Punishment of Treason, but no Attainder of Treason shall work Corruption of Blood, or Forfeiture except during the Life of the Person attainted.

ARTICLE IV.
Relations Among the States
Section 1.
Full Faith and Credit

Full Faith and Credit shall be given in each State to the public Acts, Records, and judicial Proceedings of every other State; And the Congress may by general Laws prescribe the manner in which such Acts, Records and Proceedings shall be proved, and the Effect thereof.

Section 2.
Rights of State Citizens; Right of Extradition

1. The Citizens of each State shall be entitled to all Privileges and Immunities of Citizens in the several States.

2. A Person charged in any State with Treason, Felony, or other Crime, who shall flee from Justice, and be found in another State, shall on Demand of the executive Authority of the State from which he fled, be delivered up, to be removed to the State having Jurisdiction of the Crime.

3. [No person held to Service or Labour in one State, under the Laws thereof, escaping into another, shall, in Consequence of any Law or Regulation therein, be discharged from such Service or Labour, but shall be delivered up on Claim of the Party to whom such Service or Labour may be due.]* *

Section 3.
Admission of New States

1. New States may be admitted by the Congress into this Union; but no new State shall be formed or erected within the Jurisdiction of any other State; nor any State be formed by the Junction of two or more States, or parts of States, without the Consent of the Legislatures of the States concerned as well as of the Congress.

2. The Congress shall have Power to dispose of and make all needful Rules and Regulations respecting the territory or other Property belonging to the United States; and nothing in this Constitution shall be so construed as to Prejudice any Claims of the United States, or of any particular State.

---

*Changed by the Eleventh Amendment.

**Changed by the Thirteenth Amendment.

Section 4.

Republican Government Guaranteed

The United States shall guarantee to every State in this Union a Republican Form of Government, and shall protect each of them against Invasion; and on Application of the Legislature, or of the Executive (when the Legislature cannot be convened) against domestic Violence.

ARTICLE V.

Amendment Procedures

The Congress, whenever two thirds of both Houses shall deem it necessary, shall propose Amendments to this Constitution, or, on the Application of the Legislatures of two thirds of the several States, shall call a Convention for proposing Amendments, which, in either Case, shall be valid to all Intents and Purposes, as Part of this Constitution, when ratified by the Legislatures of three fourths of the several States, or by Conventions in three fourths thereof, as the one or the other Mode of Ratification may be proposed by the Congress; Provided that no Amendment which may be made prior to the Year One thousand eight hundred and eight shall in any Manner affect the first and fourth Clauses in the Ninth Section of the first Article; and that no State, without its Consent, shall be deprived of its equal Suffrage in the Senate.

ARTICLE VI.

Supremacy of the Constitution and Federal Laws

1. All debts contracted and Engagements entered into, before the Adoption of this Constitution, shall be as valid against the United States under this Constitution, as under the Confederation.

2. This Constitution, and the Laws of the United States which shall be made in Pursuance thereof; and all Treaties made, or which shall be made, under the Authority of the United States, shall be the supreme Law of the Land; and the Judges in every State shall be bound thereby, any Thing in the Constitution or Laws of any State to the Contrary notwithstanding.

3. The Senators and Representatives before mentioned, and the Members of the several State Legislatures, and all executive and judicial Officers, both of the United States and of the several States, shall be bound by Oath or Affirmation, to support this Constitution; but no religious Test shall ever be required as a Qualification to any Office or public Trust under the United States.

ARTICLE VII.

Ratification

The Ratification of the Conventions of nine States, shall be sufficient for the Establishment of this Constitution between the States so ratifying the Same.

Done in Convention by the unanimous consent of the States present the seventeenth day of September in the year of our Lord one thousand seven hundred and eighty seven and of the Independence of the United States of America the Twelfth. In witness whereof we have hereunto subscribed our Names,

George Washington—President
and deputy from Virginia

This constitution was adopted on September 17, 1787 by the Constitutional Convention, and was declared ratified on July 2, 1788.

Signers of the Constitution

New Hampshire

John Langdon

Nicholas Gilman

Massachusetts

Nathaniel Gorham

Rufus King

Connecticut

William Samuel Johnson

Roger Sherman

New York

Alexander Hamilton

New Jersey

William Livingston

David Brearley

William Paterson

Jonathan Dayton

Pennsylvania

Benjamin Franklin

Thomas Mifflin

Robert Morris

George Clymer

Thomas Fitzsimons

Jared Ingersoll

James Wilson

Gouverneur Morris

Delaware

George Read

Gunning Bedford, Jr.

John Dickinson

Richard Bassett

Jacob Broom

Maryland

James McHenry

Daniel of St. Tho. Jenifer

Daniel Carroll

Virginia

John Blair

James Madison, Junior

North Carolina

William Blount

Richard Dobbs Spaight

Hugh Williamson

South Carolina

John Rutledge

Charles Cotesworth Pinckney

Charles Pinckney

Pierce Butler

Georgia

William Few

Abraham Baldwin

Attest *William Jackson*
Secretary

Amendments to the Constitution

Since 1787, twenty-six amendments have been proposed by the Congress and ratified by the several states, pursuant to the fifth Article of the original Constitution.

Amendment I.

Freedom of Religion and Expression

Congress shall make no law respecting an establishment of religion, or prohibiting the free exercise thereof; or abridging the freedom of speech, or of the press, or the right of the people peaceably to assemble, and to petition the Government for a redress of grievances. (Ratified December, 1791.)

Amendment II.

Right to Bear Arms

A well regulated Militia, being necessary to the security of a free State, the right of the people to keep and bear Arms, shall not be infringed. (Ratified December, 1791.)

Amendment III.

Quartering of Soldiers

No Soldier shall, in time of peace be quartered in any house, without the consent of the Owner, nor in time of war, but in a manner to be prescribed by law. (Ratified December, 1791.)

Amendment IV.

Security From Unreasonable Searches and Seizures

The right of the people to be secure in their persons, houses, papers, and effects, against unreasonable searches and seizures, shall not be violated, and no Warrants shall issue, but upon probable cause, supported by Oath or affirmation, and particularly describing the place to be searched, and the persons or things to be seized. (Ratified December, 1791.)

Amendment V.

Rights of Due Process of Law

No person shall be held to answer for a capital, or otherwise infamous crime, unless on a presentment or indictment of a Grand Jury, except in cases arising in the land or naval forces, or in the Militia, when in actual service in time of War or public danger; nor shall any person be subject for the same offence to be twice put in jeopardy of life or limb, nor shall be compelled in any criminal case to be a witness against himself, nor be deprived of life, liberty, or property, without due process of law; nor shall private property be taken for public use without just compensation. (Ratified December, 1791.)

Amendment VI.

Right to a Fair Trial

In all criminal prosecutions, the accused shall enjoy the right to a speedy and public trial, by an impartial jury of the State and district wherein the crime shall have been committed; which district shall have been previously ascertained by law, and to be informed of the nature and cause of the accusation; to be confronted with the witnesses against him; to have compulsory process for obtaining witnesses in his favor, and to have the assistance of counsel for his defence. (Ratified December, 1791.)

Amendment VII.

Trial by Jury

In Suits at common law, where the value in controversy shall exceed twenty dollars, the right of trial by jury shall be preserved, and no fact tried by a jury shall be otherwise re-examined in any Court of the United States, than according to the rules of the common law. (Ratified December, 1791.)

Amendment VIII.

Fair Bail and Punishments

Excessive bail shall not be required, nor excessive fines imposed, nor cruel and unusual punishments inflicted. (Ratified December, 1791.)

Amendment IX.

Rights Retained by the People

The enumeration in the Constitution of certain rights shall not be construed to deny or disparage others retained by the people. (Ratified December, 1791.)

Amendment X.

Powers Reserved to States and People

The powers not delegated to the United States by the Constitution, nor prohibited by it to the States, are reserved to the States respectively, or to the people. (Ratified December, 1791.)

Amendment XI.

Limitations on Federal Courts

The Judicial power of the United States shall not be construed to extend to any suit in law or equity, commenced or prosecuted against one of the United States by Citizens of another State, or by Citizens or Subjects of any Foreign State. (Ratified February, 1795.)

Amendment XII.

Election of President

The Electors shall meet in their respective states, and vote by ballot for President and Vice President, one of whom, at least, shall not be an inhabitant of the same state with themselves; they shall name in their ballots the person voted for as President, and in distinct ballots the person voted for as Vice-President, and they shall make distinct lists of all persons voted for as President, and of all persons voted for as Vice-President, and of the number of votes for each, which lists they shall sign and certify, and transmit sealed to the seat of the government of the United States, directed to the President of the Senate;—The President of the Senate shall, in the presence of the Senate and House of Representatives, open all the certificates and the votes shall then be counted;—The person having the greatest number of votes for President, shall be the President, if such number be a majority of the whole number of Electors appointed; and if no person have such majority, then from the persons having the highest numbers not exceeding three on the list of those voted for as President, the House of Representatives shall choose immediately, by ballot, the President. But in choosing the President, the votes shall be taken by states, the representation from each state having one vote; a quorum for this purpose shall consist of a member or members from two-thirds of the states, and a majority of all the states shall be necessary to a choice. [And if the House of Representatives shall not choose a President whenever the right of choice shall devolve upon them, before the fourth day of March next following, then the Vice-President shall act as President, as in the case of the death or other constitutional disability of the President—]* The person having the greatest number of votes as Vice-President, shall be the Vice-President, if such number be a majority of the whole number of Electors appointed, and if no person have a majority, then from the two highest numbers on the list, the Senate shall choose the Vice-President; a quorum for the purpose shall consist of two-thirds of the whole number of Senators, and a majority of the whole number shall be necessary to a choice. But no person constitutionally ineligible to the office of President shall be eligible to that of Vice-President of the United States. (Ratified June, 1804.)

Amendment XIII.

Slavery Abolished

Section 1. Neither slavery nor involuntary servitude, except as a punishment for crime whereof the party shall have been duly convicted, shall exist within the United States, or any place subject to their jurisdiction.

Section 2. Congress shall have power to enforce this article by appropriate legislation. (Ratified December, 1865.)

Amendment XIV.

Equal Protection and Due Process; Citizenship Defined and Guaranteed

Section 1. All persons born or naturalized in the United States and subject to the jurisdiction thereof, are citizens of the United States and of the State wherein they reside. No State shall make or enforce any law which shall abridge the privileges or immunities of citizens of the United States; nor shall any State deprive any person of life, liberty, or property, without due process of law; nor deny to any person within its jurisdiction the equal protection of the laws.

Section 2. Representatives shall be apportioned among the several States according to their respective numbers, counting the whole number of persons in each State, excluding Indians not taxed. But when the right to vote at any election for the choice of electors for President and Vice President of the United States, Representatives in Congress, the Executive and Judicial officers of a State, or the members of the Legislature thereof, is denied to any of the male inhabitants of such State, being twenty-one years of age, and citizens of the United States, or in any way abridged, except for participation in rebellion, or other crime, the basis of representation therein shall be reduced in the proportion

*Superseded by section 3 of the Twentieth Amendment.

which the number of such male citizens shall bear to the whole number of male citizens twenty-one years of age in such State.

Section 3. No person shall be a Senator or a Representative in Congress, or elector of President and Vice President, or hold any office, civil or military, under the United States, or under any State, who, having previously taken an oath, as a member of Congress, or as an officer of the United States, or as a member of any State legislature, or as an executive or judicial officer of any State, to support the Constitution of the United States, shall have engaged in insurrection or rebellion against the same, or given aid or comfort to the enemies thereof. But Congress may by a vote of two-thirds of each House, remove such disability.

Section 4. The validity of the public debt of the United States, authorized by law, including debts incurred for payment of pensions and bounties for services in suppressing insurrection or rebellion, shall not be questioned. But neither the United States nor any State shall assume or pay any debt or obligation incurred in aid of insurrection or rebellion against the United States, or any claim for the loss or emancipation of any slave; but all such debts, obligations and claims shall be held illegal and void.

Section 5. The Congress shall have power to enforce, by appropriate legislation, the provisions of this article. (Ratified July, 1868.)

Amendment XV.

Blacks' Right to Vote

Section 1. The right of citizens of the United States to vote shall not be denied or abridged by the United States or by any State on account of race, color, or previous condition of servitude.

Section 2. The Congress shall have power to enforce this article by appropriate legislation. (Ratified February, 1870.)

Amendment XVI.

Power to Tax Incomes

The Congress shall have power to lay and collect taxes on incomes, from whatever source derived, without apportionment among the several States, and without regard to any census or enumeration. (Ratified February, 1913.)

Amendment XVII.

Popular Election of Senators

The Senate of the United States shall be composed of two Senators from each State, elected by the people thereof, for six years; and each Senator shall have one vote. The electors in each State shall have the qualifications requisite for electors of the most numerous branch of the State legislatures.

When vacancies happen in the representation of any State in the Senate, the executive authority of such State shall issue writs of election to fill such vacancies: Provided, That the legislature of any State may empower the executive thereof to make temporary appointments until the people fill the vacancies by election as the legislature may direct.

This amendment shall not be so construed as to affect the election or term of any Senator chosen before it becomes valid as part of the Constitution. (Ratified April, 1913.)

Amendment XVIII.

Prohibition of Alcoholic Beverages

[Section 1. After one year from the ratification of this article the manufacture, sale, or transportation of intoxicating liquors within, the importation thereof into, or the exportation thereof from the United States and all territory subject to the jurisdiction thereof for beverage purposes is hereby prohibited.

Section 2. The Congress and the several States shall have concurrent power to enforce this article by appropriate legislation.

Section 3. This article shall be inoperative unless it shall have been ratified as an amendment to the Constitution by the legislatures of the several States, as provided in the Constitution, within seven years from the date of the submission hereof to the States by the Congress.]* (Ratified January, 1919.)

Amendment XIX.

Female Suffrage

The right of citizens of the United States to vote shall not be denied or abridged by the United States or by any State on account of sex.

Congress shall have power to enforce this article by appropriate legislation. (Ratified August, 1920.)

*Repealed by the Twenty-First Amendment.

Amendment XX.

Changes in Terms of President and Congress

Section 1. The terms of the President and Vice President shall end at noon on the 20th day of January, and the terms of Senators and Representatives at noon on the 3d day of January, of the years in which such terms would have ended if this article had not been ratified; and the terms of their successors shall then begin.

Section 2. The Congress shall assemble at least once in every year, and such meeting shall begin at noon on the 3d day of January, unless they shall by law appoint a different day.

Section 3. If, at the time fixed for the beginning of the term of the President, the President elect shall have died, the Vice President elect shall become President. If a President shall not have been chosen before the time fixed for the beginning of his term, or if the President elect shall have failed to qualify, then the Vice President elect shall act as President until a President shall have qualified; and the Congress may by law provide for the case wherein neither a President elect nor a Vice President elect shall have qualified, declaring who shall then act as President, or the manner in which one who is to act shall be selected, and such person shall act accordingly until a President or Vice President shall have qualified.

Section 4. The Congress may by law provide for the case of the death of any of the persons from whom the House of Representatives may choose a President whenever the right of choice shall have devolved upon them, and for the case of the death of any of the persons from whom the Senate may choose a Vice President whenever the right of choice shall have devolved upon them.

Section 5. Sections 1 and 2 shall take effect on the 15th day of October following the ratification of this article.

Section 6. This article shall be inoperative unless it shall have been ratified as an amendment to the Constitution by the legislatures of three-fourths of the several States within seven years from the date of its submission. (Ratified January, 1933.)

Amendment XXI.

Repeal of Alcohol Prohibition

Section 1. The eighteenth article of amendment to the Constitution of the United States is hereby repealed.

Section 2. The transportation or importation into any State, Territory, or possession of the United States for delivery or use therein of intoxicating liquors, in violation of the laws thereof, is hereby prohibited.

Section 3. This article shall be inoperative unless it shall have been ratified as an amendment to the Constitution by conventions in the several States, as provided in the Constitution, within seven years from the date of the submission hereof to the States by the Congress. (Ratified December, 1933.)

Amendment XXII.

President Limited to Two Terms

Section 1. No person shall be elected to the office of the President more than twice, and no person who has held the office of President, or acted as President, for more than two years of a term to which some other person was elected President shall be elected to the office of the President more than once. But this Article shall not apply to any person holding the office of President when this Article was proposed by the Congress, and shall not prevent any person who may be holding the office of President, or acting as President, during the term within which this Article becomes operative from holding the office of President or acting as President during the remainder of such term.

Section 2. This article shall be inoperative unless it shall have been ratified as an amendment to the Constitution by the legislatures of three-fourths of the several States within seven years from the date of its submission to the States by the Congress. (Ratified February, 1951.)

Amendment XXIII.

Presidential Suffrage for District of Columbia

Section 1. The District constituting the seat of Government of the United States shall appoint in such manner as the Congress may direct:

A number of electors of President and Vice President equal to the whole number of Senators and Representatives in Congress to which the District would be entitled if it were a State, but in no event more than the least populous State; they shall be in addition to those appointed by the States, but they shall be considered, for the purposes of the election of President and Vice President, to be electors appointed by a State; and they shall meet in the District and perform such duties as provided by the twelfth article of amendment.

Section 2. The Congress shall have power to enforce this article by appropriate legislation. (Ratified March, 1961.)

Amendment XXIV.

Poll Tax Forbidden

Section 1. The right of citizens of the United States to vote in any primary or other election for President or Vice President, for electors for President or Vice President, or for Senator or Representative in Congress, shall not be denied or abridged by the United States or any State by reason of failure to pay any poll tax or other tax.

Section 2. The Congress shall have power to enforce this article by appropriate legislation. (Ratified January, 1964.)

Amendment XXV.

Procedures for Presidential Succession

Section 1. In case of the removal of the President from office or of his death or resignation, the Vice President shall become President.

Section 2. Whenever there is a vacancy in the office of the Vice President, the President shall nominate a Vice President who shall take office upon confirmation by a majority vote of both Houses of Congress.

Section 3. Whenever the President transmits to the President pro tempore of the Senate and the Speaker of the House of Representatives his written declaration that he is unable to discharge the powers and duties of his office, and until he transmits to them a written declaration to the contrary, such powers and duties shall be discharged by the Vice President as Acting President.

Section 4. Whenever the Vice President and a majority of either the principal officers of the executive departments or of such other body as Congress may by law provide, transmit to the President pro tempore of the Senate and the Speaker of the House of Representatives their written declaration that the President is unable to discharge the powers and duties of his office, the Vice President shall im-mediately assume the powers and duties of the office as Acting President.

Thereafter, when the President transmits to the President pro tempore of the Senate and the Speaker of the House of Representatives his written declaration that no inability exists, he shall resume the powers and duties of his office unless the Vice President and a majority of either the principal officers of the executive department or of such other body as Congress may by law provide, transmit within four days to the President pro tempore of the Senate and the Speaker of the House of Representatives their written declaration that the President is unable to discharge the powers and duties of his office. Thereupon Congress shall decide the issue, assembling within forty-eight hours for that purpose if not in session. If the Congress, within twenty-one days after receipt of the latter written declaration, or, if Congress is not in session, within twenty-one days after Congress is required to assemble, determines by two-thirds vote of both Houses that the President is unable to discharge the powers and duties of his office, the Vice President shall continue to discharge the same as Acting President; otherwise, the President shall resume the powers and duties of his office. (Ratified February, 1967.)

Amendment XXVI.

Voting Age Lowered to Eighteen

Section 1. The right of citizens of the United States, who are eighteen years of age or older, to vote shall not be denied or abridged by the United States or by any State on account of age.

Section 2. The Congress shall have power to enforce this article by appropriate legislation. (Ratified July, 1971.)

Amendment XXVII

No law varying the compensation for the services of the Senators or Representatives, shall take effect, until an election of Representatives shall have intervened. (Ratified May, 1992.)

This is the original text and section numbers. Descriptive headings have been added by editors. Passages in brackets indicate that they were changed by Amendments.

Index

Picture Credits